A SHEPHERD WITHOUT SHEEP

A SHEPHERD WITHOUT SHEEP

By

E. BOYD BARRETT

THE BRUCE PUBLISHING COMPANY
MILWAUKEE

NIHIL OBSTAT:

    JOHN A. SCHULIEN, S.T.D.
    Censor librorum

IMPRIMATUR:

    ✠ ALBERT G. MEYER
    Archiepiscopus Milwauchiensis

Nov. 4, 1955

Rosary College Dewey Classification Number: 262.14

Library of Congress Catalog Card Number: 56–6719

Introduction

I HAVE no chapel; no altar at which to offer the holiest sacrifice; no pulpit from which to preach. There is no confessional where penitents await counsel and absolution from my lips; no baptismal font where, by the sacrament of regeneration, I may give to the eternal Father another child. I am a priest, Christ's shepherd, but I have no sheep.

But though I have no sheep, the Prince of Shepherds is my Friend. He needs me; He is my divine Companion. It is His will that I should be as I am. "Christ is in me," and for me that is enough.

There are others like me, in every country throughout the world, "silenced priests" living hidden lives; hidden from the world; hidden, as far as may be, in Christ. Some are my good friends.

In the book, *Shepherds in the Mist,* which I wrote soon after my return to Christ, I told of the sufferings and the loneliness of priests who, through human weakness, or confusion of mind, or under the devastating impact of sudden fear, abandoned their duty and wandered from Christ. I appealed for sympathy for them and for prayers for them, and for loving efforts to bring about their return. I stressed the phrase: "they are still ours," making it the central thought of all I wrote.

At the time I did not know that thirty years before my book appeared, St. Pius X had summarized, in a prayer, all that I had to say. He called "stray shepherds" our brothers and urged us to pray for them, to bring them back. "Have mercy, Good Pastor," said the saint, "on any priests, our brothers, who, walking in the vanity of their own sense, have by their deplorable defection saddened Thee, and Thy beloved spouse, the Church. Grant us to bring them back to Thy embrace."

Prayers going up to heaven, in ever increasing volume, for faithless priests are wondrously fruitful. Many "stray shepherds" heed the call of Christ, who searches for them in the mist. When they see Him again their hearts are moved and they come back. Then there occurs what Luke (2:20) mystically foretold: "The shepherds returned, glorifying and praising God."

Here, I can but touch lightly on the steps to be taken by a priest in order to secure pardon and reconciliation. Usually he appeals through a bishop to Christ's vicar on earth. His appeal is carefully considered at Rome, always with compassion and mercy. When Peter is satisfied that his repentance is sincere, the priest is pardoned and receives the immense privilege of again receiving the sacraments. To some, who are thus pardoned and reconciled, Peter restores in full all priestly faculties, so that, once again, they may guide and pasture sheep. In other cases this restoration of priestly

faculties is withheld. For, sometimes, during their rebellious wanderings, priests incur responsibilities from
which even their repentance does not discharge them.
Their lot it is to remain "shepherds without sheep."

They may offer the sacrifice of the Mass, but not at
the altar; only as do the nonordained faithful. They
may preach, but not from a pulpit; only as does a
good man by his example. They are still Christ's priests,
His celibate priests, but the vestments they may wear
are not white, or gold, or red, or green, or violet, but
the drab habit of humility. What then remains of their
apostolate, if the administration of the sacraments is
denied them? Can they no longer be active soldiers
of Christ?

The apostolate that is theirs is the oldest and widest
of all, the apostolate of prayer. The Little Flower asked,
"Is not the apostolate of prayer, in a certain sense, even
greater than the apostolate of preaching?" And another
saint (who differed so much in his way of life from the
gem of Lisieux), Benedict Labré, affirmed: "God's work
is done better by constant silent prayer than by great
activity."

Though inactive under ordinary circumstances, the
shepherd without sheep will rightly use, at times, his
inseparable priestly power to absolve when the shadow
of death looms. When, as has happened, I see the victim of an accident stretched on the roadside beside his
wrecked car, I give conditional absolution. On one occasion I angered a traffic officer by removing the

covering from the face of an old Italian who had just been apparently killed. "Maybe, he is not entirely dead," I said to myself, as I absolved the poor fellow.

Only a little while ago, out in the fields, I had occasion to thank God that I was a priest. It was a particularly bright morning and the sky was perfectly clear, as I walked through the meadow, saying my rosary. Maybe it was a grace that urged me to look upward. Unconsciously I suppose, I reacted to my thoughts about the Queen of Heaven. As I looked a great mushroom cloud unfolded. The suddenness of it startled me into sensing tragedy. It could only be due to the collision of jet planes, as indeed proved to be the case. At once my lips uttered the sacred words that could forgive the sins of poor pilots about to die. Then I fell on my knees, and to make doubly sure about my intention to absolve, I repeated the formula of forgiveness. The wife and children of one of the pilots who died that morning were Catholics, and it could be that their dear one had learned from them to seek God's pardon in prayer, when facing death.

What passes in the soul of the "ghost priest," the shepherd who has no flock at all? What spiritual experiences does he have? Above all, can he still have a powerful sense of faith, though he never hears the penitent's sob of relief, nor sees the light of grace and love in human eyes as the Bread of Life touches lips at the altar rail?

Christ has ways, amazing ways with souls in every

situation, in this variegated existence of ours. Such was the knowledge of a gallant and saintly young Irish Jesuit, who died a martyr of charity, as a war chaplain, in France, in 1917. He put his idea into words shortly before he died. He wrote: "Christ has put strange thoughts into my head, and given me many lights, which, I feel, have changed my whole outlook on life" (Fr. Willie Doyle).

This sentence sums up my own experience pretty well. When you come back to Christ, not having *seen* Him for a long time, you are prone to cry out for joy, to reach out and touch Him lovingly. You begin to *find* Him here, there, everywhere. He is beside you; He is within you. You realize, with amazement and delight, the utterly real and intimately close contact with Christ that faith affords. You feel new. You understand, with St. Paul (2 Cor. 5:17): "Hence if anyone is in Christ, he is a new being, his old life has passed away, a new life has begun."

As most may suspect, Christ is very indulgent toward His returned "strays." Now and again, at least, they experience what Father Doyle experienced in visiting Christ in the tabernacle: "It is a perfect joy, a comfort and recreation, to spend an hour with Him."

It is a big change for a priest, and for his soul, when he turns away from the world in disgust and disappointment, and finds *at home* what he was really looking for, albeit with closed eyes and a stalled brain, the satisfaction and the peace that only faith can give. He is still a stumbling fellow, spoiled, and laden with the aftermath of sin, but he is not without great hope of creeping close to Christ, of gaining on Him through faith. From his wandering he has learned that "no man can advance three paces on the road to perfection, unless Jesus Christ walks beside him" (Msgr. Benson). For the shepherd without sheep *faith* is the great thing: it is everything. And if he has anything at all to say about his life that can be of interest or value to his fellow men, it is about his faith that he will talk.

It is about the wonder of faith in everyday life, as it works patently and as it works hiddenly, that I write, for it, indeed, is my chief preoccupation. But lurking in the background of my mind, as I write, there is always another preoccupation, which will often reveal itself in these pages. I refer to the spiritual well-being of those wayfarers among whom I lived so long in the mist, shepherds still astray. In their behalf, what prayer is too long? What sacrifice too great? What charity too warm? They are our brothers. "Good Pastor, grant us to bring them back!"

Contents

A SHEPHERD WITHOUT SHEEP

CHAPTER I

A TRUE WORD

THE letter came at last. It came from overseas — from Rome — from Peter. It was a long time coming. So it seemed, at least. The waiting for it was a desert of anxious days.

Every repentant priest knows what it means to tear open and read that letter. His hands tremble as he scans Latin sentences that will tell him if he is to live or to die. Then, he smiles his *Deo Gratias,* as I did. And the penance that, on re-reading, he discovers to be imposed upon him, however considerable it may be, only tends to deepen his joy. The penance somehow reassures him that Peter was not asleep when he decided on pardon.

The repentant priest makes his confession soon after. For that confession he may need the long list of sins at the back of his prayer book to help refresh his memory. "I'm a priest and it's about twenty years since my last confession, Father!" That's how I began! But my mind was less occupied with the trouble of telling my sins, than with the anticipated joy of the coming morning and the Bread of Life.

The days that followed were April weather, sunshine and showers. Now clouds would cross the sky, some fears, some uncertainties. Was I really sincere, really in earnest? Could I, would I persevere? In a sense I was floundering in the present, with a past that made me shudder, and a future that looked, somehow, forbidding. And, besides, I had not as yet a firm grip on prayer.

It became known in time, in the Catholic world around New York, that I had made my submission to Rome and had been mercifully pardoned, and many a kind heart rejoiced.

Letters began to pour in on me, saying in a hundred different ways: "Welcome home!" They were warm, happy letters, and many of them told of prayers and sacrifices offered for me during the period that I was "away." Those letters encouraged me and I was grateful for them. But among them all there was one that became an immense help and inspiration to me. It was written by a complete stranger, a lady who lived alone in a big house in New York.

The lady, after modestly and graciously welcoming me back to the Church, wrote this little sentence: "*Now there is nothing between you and Christ!*" Seemingly commonplace, this message went straight to my heart. No doubt it came laden with grace. There was goodness, and wisdom, and prayer behind it. It was "A True Word" — a word with spiritual life in it!

Not long after, I happened to make an afternoon visit to the parish church of this locality. I confess that I was not in a devout mood and I was far from enjoying that comforting *feeling* of a lively faith. So, when I entered and genuflected, I took a seat close to the door. The church was empty; that is, there was no other *mere human* there.

I tried to pray as I knelt but my mind wandered. I was back at school once again. I was fifteen. I was in County Kildare. I was seeing the face of a saintly priest whom I knew and liked, Father John. And now he was here by my side — it was California once more and not Kildare — and he was whispering to me and his hand was under my elbow. He was using my school name, as he said: "Nearer, Jack, nearer!"

It was plain what Father John meant. I should not remain near the door, at the back of the church, but I should be up at the altar rail, close to Christ. As I rose and moved forward, the saint's hand seemed to urge me on gently until I reached a point, near as could be to the tabernacle. He left me there to pray, within breathing distance of Christ.

Suddenly prayer became easy. I was now doing exactly as Christ asked me to do, when He said: "Come to Me!" What startling light there is in grasping the meaning of some simple utterance of Jesus!

I had not seen before the import of those three words: "Come to Me!" "Sure," I told myself, "He wants me near Him — not far away, back at the door!" I wasn't fit or ready in any way to be so near Christ. But what of it? He had not said: "As soon as you are fit and ready (and feel pious) come to Me!" Just as I am, *hic et nunc,* that's the way He wants me!

As I prayed, "the true word" that the New York lady had written to me came to mind. *"Now there is nothing between you and Christ!"* Christ seemed to know what was in my mind — as of course He did — and asked my soul: "Why not be good friends with Me?"

It was that afternoon that the first dawning of a new insight into prayer lit up my mind. I began to understand that in prayer, words are not important, nor thoughts, nor the comprehension of what's happening, nor devout imaginings and feelings. But there is an utterly objective fact that is important, that has immense value. It is proximity to Christ, either physical proximity or proximity by faith alone. When one is close to Christ, when one is touching Him, there comes from Him a virtue that heals. And one has the right to creep up close to Christ, at any time, in any place, for He has promised not to drive away anyone who comes to Him.

I am conscious, as I write, that I have been describing a somewhat intimate scene between an unfaithful priest and Christ, whom he betrayed. It is a scene, *mutatis mutandis*, of not infrequent occurrence. And, in revealing my personal secret, I am revealing the secret of other priests who, like me, fled from the tragedy of sacrilege. It is a scene in that divine drama — that angels watch, exulting — in which Christ plays the role of hero and lover, in winning a soul.

In this book, I have to tell of some of those passages between Christ and me, some of those contacts and exchanges, that put me plainly on record as witness that Christ is divine, and is active among us. I do not know into what hands such a book as this may fall. It may perchance be read by someone of little or of no faith who will say: "See! It is because this man wants to believe in Christ that he believes!"

It is true that I want to believe in Christ. I want to believe in Him more and more each day. But the reason that that want exists in my heart is that I know what it is to believe: I know the richness and value of faith; that it is, as Peter said, "much more precious than gold" (1 Pet. 1:7).

Do we believe only because we want to believe? What if, through momentary darkness of soul, we wished to be without faith? Can anyone, even a priest, strive to discard the faith, to be rid of it — and yet fail in his evil effort?

Some months ago, in the midst of a great storm, a priest in sore distress, a straying shepherd, came to visit me. He was a young Irishman of powerful build and his story was full of sorrow. There was one thing he told me that gave tragic testimony to the deathlessness of his faith, as it did to the depth of his fall. He told me how, not wanting to do evil, but being in despair of avoiding it, he had prayed that his faith might die! In mercy, God refused his request. Nothing could kill his faith! As humbly together we said a few *Ave Marias*, the tears rolled down his cheeks.

It is surely beyond human comprehension that the

faith should survive the terrible thing that a priest does
when he abandons Christ.

> O Christ, O Ruler of Battles,
> Woe to him that deserts his mighty Lord!
> (Book of Lismore, A.D. 1411.)

But the ways of God's mercy are unfathomable, and in
spite of all, the wandering priest's faith survives. I have
personally met and known a number of them, but never,
save possibly in two cases, had I reason to doubt about
their faith.

They may, in earning their daily bread, be salesmen,
or opera singers, or radio repair men, or photographers,
or even bouncers in taverns; they may be virtual hoboes,
"from table to table wandering with a gang of villains"
(*ibid.*), but always they are different from other men,
and the deathless spiritual experience of having once
offered the Sacrifice of Calvary survives in their hearts.
The priest's faith remains because he can never unlive
the Mass!

When at length, after the miseries of exile are over,
he returns, the priest becomes in a special way "a
witness of the Church," because he has triumphed over
the direst trial that faith can be put to. He has dwelt
for a long period in a dreary cabin of the devil's motel.
He has seen and heard the worst blasphemies against
Christ, and yet he returns to tell a unique spiritual experience of the power, the love, the presence of Christ. In
the repentant priest's soul Christ has continued His
revelation.

In his book, *Jesus and His Times*, Daniel-Rops writes: "For two thousand years an incalculable number of men and women have testified to the Presence (of Christ) as the most certain of realities." Men lacking in learning and in solid virtue tell of it as well as the Bernards, Bonaventures, and Aquinases. Even the babes and sucklings of scholarship and sanctity confess their secret knowledge of the most certain of realities.

"It is not only the saints who can surprise in themselves, if only dimly and almost by stealth, this secret knowledge" (*ibid.*). Looking back on his experiences of escapes from wrong-doing and of inspirations to do good, every shepherd without sheep can, I think, remember occasions when, had he known the words, he would have said with St. Bernard, "He was closer to me than I myself."

CHAPTER II

MOORINGS OF FAITH

WHEN a priest "comes home" and settles down, it is a happy, wonderful experience for him to be trusted again by those whom he respects and loves. Now he has what most of all things he yearned for, and it is for him a kind of heaven. Having known what it means to have to hide from his best friends, to be forever escaping from hunting, haunting thoughts, it is good to meet the eyes of well-wishers with a frank glance and to be glad.

The trust and confidence shown me has taken many forms, and it was never tardy. Money was freely given me to be spent on priests whom I knew to be still in distress. Mothers and sisters wrote to me about their sons or brothers "out there," imploring my advice and help. Magazines gladly accepted my articles, though they must have thought them old-fashioned. A good Benedictine father invited me to co-operate in his book on Catholic authors and even suggested, to my amazement, that I should be included in his list. The late Father Daniel Lord, S.J., called on me for two pamphlets. My pastor gave me the key to his sacristy and welcomed me as his Mass server. In letters I was consulted for advice in difficult and delicate problems. Among other curious displays of good will, a missioner, about to return to his obscure corner of the faraway Indies, visited me, just to see me and to shake my hand. And more than one grand old pastor, worn with toil in Christ's service, has knelt at my feet to ask *my* blessing!

All that trust should have built up in me a humble and reasonable self-confidence — the "fear not" spirit that Christ told us to have — but, alas, though it helped, it fell short of helping me enough. I had discovered within myself a something that I thought could never be cured. I seemed to myself to be hurt and spoiled forever. Had not the stain of treason rotted the very fibers of my heart? Inaudible to everyone but to myself, I would whisper Shakespeare's words: "Treason is trusted like a fox."

Why did I not realize then, as I do now, that there is no inner hurt to mind or soul or character that lies beyond Christ's healing power? Why did I not understand that the virtue that derives from being with Christ cures everything and everyone — and if everyone, then also me? It was my faith that my "incurable malady" was disturbing and perhaps undermining.

It must be recalled that for twenty years I had lived a life of spiritual treachery, facing from day to day the hopeless, impossible task of quieting, by sophistry, an uneasy protesting conscience. I lectured, I wrote, with my tongue in my cheek. I hated to mislead others, but I misled them and I misled myself. Pretending to be "a Catholic in good standing," and one who still cherished the ancient faith, I set about exposing what I called "the faults of my church" — faults that were fabrications of my imagination and my ignorance. Though hating and despising agnosticism, I made agnostics my friends and was charmed by their flattery. This horrid masquerade of deceit, that lasted for so many years, could not but sully and ruin my sense of honor and truth. It soiled me and left an ugly mark, a stain, in my character. I came, in time, to recognize myself as wholly lacking in sincerity, as unreliable, as one whose mind as well as soul was badly hurt.

Could such a one ever again be capable of that honest, truthful certainty that belongs to men of honor? How could my mind, my character be healed? How recover a faith that had no anxiety, no distress in it — that sense of pure friendship with Christ that precludes even the faintest shade of doubt?

It was in a strange illogical way that my problem was solved, but what mattered the lack of logic when the cure worked? It is hard for me to explain what exactly happened but, in general, it was as follows.

Figuratively, I was like a boat in a stormy sea, drifting toward danger, and then, suddenly, I discovered that the drifting was only apparent because I was safely held by two moorings.

The two moorings that I discovered were two unshakeable convictions that emerged from the depths of my mind. In their presence I could no longer worry about the sincerity of my faith.

The first conviction derived from the need I felt to be of help to others, to my fellow men, my brothers. This spiritual yearning was, no doubt, a grace, God's blessing in my heart. Those in need, near or far, high or low, foe or friend, had to be helped, and it was compulsory on me to do it. God had put love in my heart, and life was love. I was powerless and poor, but God's love compelled me to believe in the possibility of assisting others, no matter where they were or who they were. What was seemingly impossible was somehow possible. I wanted to help Christ's vicar in Rome. I wanted to help poor Teresa, a bedridden arthritic in Dublin. I wanted to help Pat, "a disabled veteran" of the ranks of the priesthood. I longed to lend my aid to the aging Archbishop of Melbourne and a gallant cripple in a home in London, England. There were scores of others that I had to assist, and there were institutes and causes to which I had to give generously. Such was my first conviction, but how was it possible for me to spread out my nonexistent resources?

There had to be some Great Helper, some Mighty Giver, some Divine Fool of Love to make my dreams come true! There had to be Christ! Without Christ the God-given compulsion in me to help others could not be satisfied. Christ had to be as I believed Him to be: a Man, limitlessly good, infinitely divine.

In my hours of worry an old and solid piece of Christian philosophy would emerge and hold the focus of my mind. It could be formulated in a few words:

"Without Christ, life here below could have no meaning." I would, at times, picture the world as a vast area of darkness, sadness, and confusion. Men living aimless lives, driven to despair by hate and pride and sin. Innocence nowhere; trust nowhere; and peace unknown. Hearts languishing in the fear and horror of living in a Christless world! How could I face an existence among soulless men, among beings who had no higher hope? To me, the impossibility, the monstrosity, of a Christless world was evident. There had to be Christ. I had to have Christ. Christ was as I believed Him to be!

That was my second conviction, a certainty rooted deep in my heart. I had only to renew consciousness of these two personal convictions to recover renewed confidence in the purity and solidity of my faith, and to realize how securely moored it was. How groundless were my worries about the quality of my faith!

But there remained something to do to clinch my victory. I had to associate my little triumph with Christ Himself. So I came to Him, in that frank and simple way that He wants us to come to Him, and I told Him how disturbed I had been, and then I asked Him to answer me plainly and, as it were, "on His honor," if my faith in Him was really genuine and sincere, and also if my love for Him was really genuine and sincere.

His voice came to me, not through my ears, but through invisible portals of my heart. It came gentle as where the blue-gray of the sky meets the vanishing sea — entrancing as that moving, unseen breeze that rushes through oak leaves so hastelessly — and it said: "Your love is sincere and true! Your faith is sincere and true!" How happy that divine message made me! It was all I wanted to know!

A shepherd without sheep has time aplenty to ruminate on things and "Christ puts strange thoughts into his head." In the back of his memory there are echoes of the raucous cry he heard in the wilderness: "Christ is not divine! Christ is not divine." He thinks about the dull-eyed men who kept on repeating the lie, in the hope, through long repetition, of making it credible. But he recalls that the men who utter blasphemies against Christ do so at a great distance from Him. They refuse to meet Him, to accept His invitation: "Come and see!" They betray their fear of learning about Christ, of coming under His influence, of experiencing His goodness.

Pondering on this, the shepherd without sheep sees that true and deep faith is not to be won by the mere repetition of prayers and hymns that acknowledge Christ's divinity, but rather by an actual approach to Christ, a "coming to see Him," a "watching with Him," a "reaching forth of the hand to touch Him," a coming under His influence and an intimate experiencing of His goodness.

I have had experience of people, "anxious Catholics" I call them, who allow themselves, perhaps inadvertently, to worry over the spiritual safety — the perseverance — of others.

Frankly and plainly, it is impossible for us, poor weak

mortals, to foretell with certainty whether or not we shall persevere. It is true that Christ told Dismas all would be well with him, poor thief. But Christ did that only a little while before Dismas was killed.

Christ will not tell us, in so many words, that we shall win our way to Paradise. None of us can claim to be "saved"; but, on the other hand, none of us should distrust Christ's will to save us. I think we should love Him all the more and bless Him all the more, for keeping us in the dark about our eternal future. It's wise to love what Christ does and the way He does it. But what about the anxious Catholic? And what about his or her attitude toward a shepherd without sheep?

Once a good nun, an old friend by correspondence, wrote to me out of the fullness of a pious (but anxious) heart: "I won't be happy about you until I know that you are in a Trappist monastery." Apparently it did not cross her mind that it might not be the right thing for me to become a Trappist. It is not the location of a soul, even among a community of saints, that is most important for the soul, but obedience to God's will. My friend no doubt meant, though she did not write it, "I won't be happy about you until I know that you are where your ecclesiastical superior wishes you to be!"

A few priests who happily emerge from "the mist" do take refuge in Trappist monasteries. I know one such, a man of great goodness and gifted, as it seems, with the power to mind-read from a distance. He writes to me when he can and I value his letters more than I can tell. Of late (it was after I had been ill) he wrote:

Dear Boyd,

I have been thinking of you considerably the past week. I am wondering whether you are ill. Generally, when I have someone on my mind, I start praying intensively for that individual for I feel prayers are needed. Never a day . . . sometimes several times a day . . . but I pray for you. I just love to pray for those I love. . . . When you are alone with the Master whisper a wee prayer for me. . . . Help me to save my soul. . . . You can obtain the grace I need to become a saint, a little saint at least. . . .

(*signed*) A.

Father A's saying, "I love to pray for those I love," is his way of expressing the first of those two convictions of mine, recounted above. Father A feels the urgent need to help others; and he sees in prayer, that is in Christ, the only way and the sure way of helping others. Father A's heart is big; he loves all his fellow men; he prays for all, for his faith has no bounds. He feels, he knows as I do, that life can have no meaning without Christ. His cell, his chapel, his cloister, his library, and the fields where he works with his brother monks, are all for him redolent of Christ.

In Father A, the Good Shepherd has back in His arms, and all His, a priest once listed as a "casualty."

Chapter III

A LITTLE GIFT

I CAN see that a big change has come over me as the aftermath of my "home-coming" and my lonely vocation as a priest whose hands are tied and whose lips are sealed. The change came about gradually and yet not slowly. I'm glad of it and I think it makes a story which, if I can relate it aright, will be of interest.

In the background of my story I see the early years of my busy fervor as a Catholic lad who loved his vocal prayers and his devotions. I aimed at doing good by my example, by frequent approach to the sacraments, visits to the tabernacle, giving what alms I could to the poor, and making what efforts I could to convert sinners and non-Catholics. My ideal was the missioner, and above all the missioner-martyr, dying to win pagan souls to God. I saw virtue in terms of activity, of doing things for God. My eyes rested lovingly (and exclusively, I think) on external activity spent in the great cause. What Paul wrote to Timothy (2 Tim. 4:2) expressed my dream: "Preach the word; be instant in season, out of season; reprove, entreat, rebuke in all patience and doctrine."

Even when I entered religion, submitting willingly

16

and co-operatively to my training, my viewpoint remained unchanged. I thought of myself as getting ready
for really efficient external work. My studies would make
me a great preacher and writer and apologist. I promised
myself "to wear myself out" in external labor for Christ,
the while by prayer and obedience I grew in virtue.
Always I was longing "to get going," to be doing things.
I don't think that my purpose and outlook were other
than good and honest. But was there not, all the same,
something wrong somewhere?

It is not easy to pinpoint the faultiness of my philosophy of religion, otherwise than to say that I was
overemphasizing the importance of action, of doing
things. I was, though not consciously, assuming that
God really needed the crack of my rifle and the thrust
of my bayonet, in order to win His battle. Instead of
saying to God: "With Your help I'll try to do what
You want, whether it be to work or to rest in idleness,"
I said to God: "Dear God, I'm going to do this and
that for You! See if I don't!" Poor fool, I was a victim
of self-expression in its most childish form!

But, the reader will ask, had I no exercise in con-
templation? No attraction for silent adoration? No experience of the meaning of the presence of God?

Well, of course, I meditated faithfully every day, and
I spent my holy hours in pious adoration, but always
I was impatient to get away to work. I admired those
who, like Carmelite nuns, tried to live in the presence
of God, but I thought that the practice was unnatural

and virtually impossible. I didn't understand what it meant. I felt sure it was not for me; in fact, that I would "break my head" if I attempted it.

How is it that I did not see that the devil was fooling me? He was, in effect, encouraging me to keep at a little distance from Christ. I heard the devil advising: "Don't go too near Him! It would be too much for you! Keep at least fifty yards away!" And whenever I heard Christ calling to me to come up close to Him, to come into His presence, I was somehow reluctant to do so. I loved Christ — but I was afraid to go near Him! Sure! I'd work for Him — I'd work hard! But, no, thanks! I wouldn't lie down to sleep at His feet!

For years, then, the devil deceived me into regarding myself as quite important to God, and as having the right to decide upon the type of co-operation that I would give to God. Then something happened, that the devil cannot have liked at all. The something was a little gift that came to me unexpectedly, and that had, as a result, something very important for me. I got wise to the evil one's game. That lady who lived alone in a big house in New York, and who had told me in her wonderful letter: "Now there is nothing between you and Christ," sent me a book of 127 pages, entitled: *Practice of the Presence of God,* by a poor French Carmelite lay brother, Nicholas Herman (1607–1691).* It was a little gift in one respect; it was a very big gift in another. Brother Lawrence, as Herman was

---

* The Newman Press, Westminster, Md., 1947.

called in religion, told me as I read how he had discovered "the shortest and easiest way" to holiness. And his discovery was no fake!

Brother Lawrence, who in his early days had been for a brief time a soldier and adventurer, was a simple, upright fellow, blunt and outspoken, but invariably affable and kind. He worked as cook and cobbler in his community in Paris, but on account of his shrewdness he was, at times, entrusted with such important business as selecting and buying wine for the monastery. He gradually gained a great reputation for wisdom and virtue. He was often consulted by outsiders and left behind him a few spiritual notes which, together with a few letters that he wrote, are his only relics. As the years went by, and as he won his way through great spiritual crises, he developed what we may call a "one-track mind" in religion. He spoke and wrote and thought only of the presence of God. He lived with God everywhere and always, but in a very human, lovable, natural way. "I possess God," he wrote, "as tranquilly in the bustle of my kitchen as if I were on my knees before the Blessed Sacrament." His faith was so strong and so vivid that it became for him a kind of knowledge; a seeing, hearing, feeling, a faith of utter realism. "I live," he said, "as though there were no one but God and me in the world. . . . God is nearer to us than we think. . . . Faith makes me touch God with my finger."

Brother Lawrence had an independent spirit. He did not hesitate, prayerfully, to think things out for him-

self. He found the right answers without seeking much
for guidance from spiritual directors. He was not afraid
to say: "If you wish to make progress in the spiritual
life, pay no attention to the fine words or the elegant
discourses of the learned of this world. Bad luck to those
who try to satisfy their curiosity with the learning of
men. It is the Creator who teaches truth." Brother
Lawrence acquired the habit of talking directly to God,
and therein he found peace. "If we wish to enjoy, even
in this life the peace of Paradise, we must accustom
ourselves to familiar, humble, and loving intercourse with
God." The time came when this intimate converse with
God so occupied him that he had no time for the devotions that others find useful and comforting. "I have
given up," he wrote, "all my private devotions and
prayers which are not of obligation, and occupy myself
only with holding myself ever in God's holy presence."

As I read Brother Lawrence, I found a lively interest
awaken when he began to show that his practice of
remaining near Christ was easy, natural, and within the
reach of all. He had detected in himself an inability to
meditate. He had, he confesses, been scared by certain
advanced theories of spirituality that he had heard of;
but he hit on the fact that "neither skill nor knowledge
were needed to go to God," and that to do so was easy.

"This exercise does not kill the body," he wrote. It
is for everyone; the ignorant, the weak, the helpless.
No effort, no strain, no special "posture" was called for;
just to glance upward to God; to speak to God; to be

glad to be near Him. "In the way of God thoughts count for little: love does everything. . . . God insensibly lights divine fire in the soul." Brother Lawrence recommended this as "the holiest, the firmest, the easiest, and the most efficacious manner of prayer."

One can, perhaps, summarize the inner meaning and the essential value of the practice of the presence of God in four words: *"Faith grows by faith."*

There was one sentence Brother Lawrence wrote that made me (as I thought back on the years of my active priesthood) recognize what opportunities of doing good I had lost, both as preacher and confessor. The sentence deserves to be printed on cards to be hung in every presbytery.

"If I were a preacher I would preach nothing else than the practice of the presence of God; if I were a director of souls, I would urge it upon everyone, so necessary and even easy do I believe it to be."

His faith was, of course, Brother Lawrence's mainstay. "Oh faith, faith!" he used to cry aloud, as tears filled his eyes. He valued and loved his faith above all else. To his faith he owed everything. "By faith," he wrote, "I learn more about God in a short time than I would learn in many years in the schools."

"Faith sees by the ears," says an old proverb, and in Lawrence's case, as he heard God speaking in his heart, he saw Him.

When Brother Lawrence complained of his inability to meditate, it may have been that he experienced a kind of impatience with it. Perhaps he thought that it was more profitable to his soul to rest in intimate union with God, "speaking familiarly with Him," to use his own words, than to sit as it were studying (from a distance, in student fashion) some aspect of God's power or of Christ's activity. He had Christ with him in his kitchen or beside him on his cobbler's bench, just as Thérèse found Christ "amid the pots and pans," and it would have been quite a jolt for him to set about a *compositio loci* (as in formal meditation), and *imagine* Christ doing something far away in the distant past. Though meditation stirs up holy purposes and furnishes the mind with inspiring thoughts, it is not a satisfactory substitute for union with God.

For myself, though I meditated daily, an hour a day, for twenty years of religious life (obeying the rules of meditating as well as I could), I failed to learn from this method of prayer the meaning and practice of the presence of God. Christ was within me: I was carrying Christ, but I did not appreciate that fact. Like St. Bernard's ass was I. "The ass which carried our Lord did not cease to be an ass," the saint said.

Cardinal Mercier, whose faith was as simple and direct as any poor turf cutter in the Bog of Allen, wrote: "Reality is God dwelling within us. Many baptized souls are ignorant of this mystery and remain their whole lives unaware of it. . . . The very people whose mission it is to preach it throughout the world, neglect it, forget it, and when it is brought home to them are astonished."

How comes it that we can carry God in our hearts without adverting to that fact? "Is it that you carry Me within you and do not know it?" (St. Bernard.) And, if we do advert to the fact, should it frighten us? Are we not God's children? Do children feel fear when their father is at hand?

The response of St. Elizabeth of the Holy Trinity to the realization of God's presence was something other than fear. "I have found my heaven on earth," she said, "for heaven is God and God is in my soul." St. Elizabeth was unconsciously stealing from St. Augustine, when she expressed that comforting thought, for the Bishop had written long before her time: "We are heaven . . . in virtue of carrying the God of heaven, we are heaven."

On all of us, sinners and wanderers alike, the sense of God's presence has a unique effect. It makes us bow our heads, be still, and adore. The angels watch and listen. Now all fear disappears. There is nothing to be afraid of, nothing to bewail!

When, as happens, a priest who has lost his bearings comes to talk to me, and maybe join me in a drive along and above the shore, we stop where the sea breaks against a headland. We notice, consciously or unconsciously, that "the earth is full of the majesty of God's glory" and we pray a while. Sometimes the whole Rosary; sometimes only a decade. Then returning, still near the sea, we pass the place where the Dominican

Sisters take care of the sick. In the little chapel there I have knelt with "strays" and noticed their deathlike stillness, their bowed heads, their adoration.

Coming from the chapel we pass a white robe and she stops to say a word. God is here again behind her kind, quiet eyes. I hear my friend breathing fast.

She may know me and inquire: "A nice cool glass of lemonade?"

I say: "You didn't think, maybe, of something a lot stronger?"

The smile. A good nun's smile! And now my friend smiles.

It could be that the confusion is a little less in another stray's mind; that his heart is reopening for Christ to enter it again. "There within am I to be found by whoever finds me" (St. Bernard).

CHAPTER IV

I TOUCH CHRIST

LIKE those who surrounded Christ while He was on earth, I touch Him. I act as though I were one of the crowd that Luke (6:19) described: "All the multitude sought to touch him, for virtue went out from him and healed all." I do not touch Him in order to reassure myself of His reality. Of that, there is no doubt at all in my mind. I touch Him instinctively, because He is so good, and because there is great gain in doing so. There is, however, an added reason why I touch Christ. It is really the most important reason of all. I touch Him because He told me to do so.

When He said to Thomas, at the famous post-resurrection scene: "Reach hither your hand. . . ." or "Let me have thy hand" as Msgr. Knox translates it. . . . He was not speaking to the shame-faced Apostle alone, but to me also. In plain words Christ invites me to touch Him and I do so. It increases my faith; it heals my soul.

When Christ said to me: "Let Me have thy hand," He made it clear to me that He does not want me to be afraid of Him and to keep at a distance from Him. Those who shy away from Christ hurt Him. Why should we fear to approach Him? Is He not awfully good and kind? And has He not reassured us (in case we should approach Him with sins on our souls, as indeed is most likely): "He who comes to Me I will not drive away"?

When I say, as I do, that I touch Christ, what do I mean exactly? Do I mean that I touch Christ physically with my hand as, for example, I pat the graying head of my dog Bran and feel his affectionate reaction?

No! I do not and cannot touch Christ in that way. Though He is close to me now, He is beyond my physical reach. As St. Thomas says: *"Visus, tactus, gustus, in Te fallitur.* Sight, touch, taste fail me in finding You."

Do I mean then when I say, I touch Christ, that I imagine with vividness that I touch Him? Am I speaking poetically of a poetic vision in which, for example, my arms entwine the sacred feet of Christ?

No, again! Imagination, fancy, poetic vision has nothing whatever to do with the contact, the real contact, that I can enjoy with Christ. Though through some brain surgery all my imaginative faculty were removed and all sensitivity destroyed, I could still touch Christ.

My power to touch Christ derives from the divine gift of faith. This power transcends the natural; this power is more real than any mere natural power.

"How can we touch Christ, now that He has ascended into heaven?" asks St. Augustine. Answering, he says: "He touches Christ who believes in Him." We recall what Brother Lawrence said: "Faith makes me touch God with my finger."

The act of touching has deep significance. A mother smooths her child's fevered brow and brings instant relief. A friend takes a friend by the hand in a firm grasp and two hearts meet. The returning prodigal saw his father coming to meet him, but he knew love and repentance only when his father took him in his embrace. Even a dog will respond in a deep, pathetic way to the feel of his master's hand.

My Irish setter Bran, wanting to be always near me, seems to have given me all his heart. He follows me everywhere; his soft brown eyes, thoughtful and trusting, watch me. He is at my feet when I sit reading in a chair. If I drive off in my car leaving him behind, he howls in despair. Every night, as I turn off the lights, saying: "Go to sleep now, Bran!" he looks at me, doleful and aggrieved.

Sometimes when he falls asleep at my feet I notice his feet stir in rhythm, as in his dream he chases a hare through distant fields. Soon he awakens, tilts back his head, and opens wide his eyes to stare at me in bewilderment. There is anxiety in his eyes for he has lost me in his dream, and now, though he sees me again, he doubts if I am real. He is confused; he needs to be reassured.

There is a way, a sure way, to bring back comfort to Bran's anxious eyes. "Give me your paw, Bran!" I say, leaning toward him. After a little pause, he raises his paw and plunges it, flat and heavy, into my hand. That way he finds me again, and knows that I am real. His eyes brighten in a steady, fixed glance and he lies back content, to watch and doze. What, more than touch, makes reality *real?*

The instinct to touch things that are precious or gentle or beautiful is common to us all. By touching a thing we possess it in some way, at least momentarily. Often children, passing by my car, stand to watch Bran, seated in the back, with his friendly old head poked through the window. They love his gentle brown eyes, and they talk to him. As they come nearer, they say to me: "Please, may I touch him?" and they stretch up their little hands, unafraid.

I know how they feel. Long ago as a child of four or five, when I was in our garden at home, I saw to my surprise and delight a pretty dove perched in an apple tree. It was quite near me, and I noticed a kind of purple ring around its neck. It seemed very gentle as well as pretty, and I felt I wanted to put my hand on it and pet it.

There was a low branch on the tree and it was easy to climb, so I stole over and began to make my way up. The dove, to my delight, did not fly away but stayed watching me — not a bit afraid. Soon I had my hand on its back, stroking it. Then I lifted it up caressingly, and pressed it to me as I descended the tree and brought it into the house. It was mine! I got a large cage for it and I had it as my well-fed little friend for years. It was my first happy experience in the world's old philosophy: "Touch and take!"

Mothers crowded round the good Christ, when He was on earth. They pushed their little ones in front of them so that they might touch Christ and He them. He was glad to take them in His arms; to possess them, at least momentarily. Christ was prone to allow His human instinct to have its way. He would touch blind eyes to give back sight — "Then he touched their eyes saying: According to your faith be it done unto you. And their eyes were opened" (Mt. 9:29, 30). He would take the hand of a sick old woman or a young girl who had just died and health or life would return — "He went in and took her by the hand and the maid arose" (Mt. 9:25).

And Christ allowed Himself to be robbed of favors. He suffered Himself to be the victim of "Touch and Take." There was that very sick woman who had watched Christ and who believed in His power — "She said within herself: If I shall touch only His garment I shall be healed" (Mt. 9:21). This holy felony did not anger Christ. He let the woman keep what she had taken — and indeed praised her faith.

When we want something badly and in a hurry — some grace, some spiritual favor, some healing for our sick souls — would it not be proper for us to touch Christ and to take from Him what we want? Did He not offer Himself as a willing victim by saying to us, as plainly as He did, "Reach hither your hand! Let me have your hand!"

I am making no reference to many explicit (and implicit) instances in the Gospel where Christ, in His lovably human way, touched the poor or suffered them to touch Him. He allowed friends to embrace Him, and foes to buffet Him, and made no complaint. Only on one occasion (Jn. 20:17) did He utter four startling words, and those to one of His dearest friends: "Do not touch Me!" Here, the plain Christian, who is no scholar in exegesis, may ask for a word of explanation.

The occasion was the sudden and delirious recognition of the risen Christ by Magdalen. It happened a few feet away from the tomb. Crying "Rabboni!" she had flung herself at His feet, clinging to Him. She was beside herself in the ecstasy of her joy. She felt she could never let go hold of her Master again. In fact, she forgot herself; forgot an urgent and important duty that was obligatory upon her, that of hastening to tell Peter and the other Apostles about the good news.

Christ loved Magdalen. He had rejoiced to have her kneel, clinging at His feet in former times. But now He had to bring her to her senses. Jesus uttered the seemingly harsh words: "Do not touch Me!" meaning perhaps, "Do not now be clinging to Me!" in order to save Magdalen from a dereliction of her duty.

The four words "Do not touch Me" (*Noli me tangere*) were not meant for me. I touch Christ because of those other words that were meant for me: "Reach hither your hand!"

CHAPTER V

WHEN IS A MIRACLE?

A NUMBER of priests, and I hear, bishops as well, read detective stories, and I do too. The best of them are clean and robust. I read them at night because they do not keep me awake as books of science do. I have learned something from them, something that in an indirect way has helped my faith. The great detectives of fiction have taught me to be cautious about accepting coincidences, so called, as due to mere chance, rather than to design. When in a plot I read of some strange, unexpected happening, I am slow to regard it as a coincidence. And now, in actual life, the pattern holds. When something strange and wonderful occurs, I think twice before I eliminate Providence and say: "It's just chance!" Rather, I am inclined to call it a "little miracle."

Catholics are regarded by many as credulous people, ready to believe, to swallow anything. But should we not rather be praised for our inquisitiveness, our scientific attitude? We refuse to accept right away the explanation of a mysterious, seemingly supernatural, incident as mere coincidence. We are (with the great detectives of fiction) inclined to suspect that there is design behind the incident, and not mere chance. Looking at the elaborate plot of my life I find that there are just too many coincidences in it. Frankly, I am utterly unable to attribute all of the little miracles I've been involved in as due to natural causes.

Going back to my childhood for a moment, I was a frequent witness of astonishing little incidents. My mother who was really good and beautiful had what should be called an extraordinary devotion to St. Anthony of Padua. She loved him; thought him wonderful; and certainly it seemed to me that he was very wonderful to her. He never, as far as I could see, refused her anything. She'd often lose things, earrings or brooches or keys or important papers; then she'd kneel and pray, often asking me to join with her. A few minutes later what she had lost turned up.

Through the years I'm sure I witnessed fifty or a hundred of these favors, as my mother called these unprovable little miracles. I doubt, as I look back, if any great detective unraveling the plot of my mother's life would have been satisfied that they were just coincidences.

My mother entrusted us, her three little boys, to the protection of St. Anthony. So what? Well, for instance . . .

One day my brother Joe and I were coming back from the chapel under the care of our old nurse. He was over four years at the time, and I was a year younger. He was a chubby, handsome boy, skipping and running around. At the corner, above the chapel, there was a big tavern, a public house, and at the curb stood a horse-drawn lorry belonging to the Guinness Brewery of Dublin. The horses were the famous Guinness Clydesdales, huge, magnificent animals. It was summer time, and the flies were annoying them, and as happens they were stamping their mighty hoofs, raising them a foot or so, and bringing them down sharply on the cobble-stoned street.

Well, as it happened, my brother slipped on the path and rolled off, until his head lay directly under the raised hoof of one of the Clydesdales. I see him there now, vividly, helpless and certain to be crushed to death. Now, what could St. Anthony do? Poor old nurse rushed over and snatched him up. By a strange coincidence she had time to do that! Then the mighty hoof of the restless horse smashed down.

I have said above, that there have been too many coincidences in my life to attribute all of them to mere chance or to natural causes. I'm prepared and willing to concede that the natural and the supernatural are often combined in producing phenomena.

There was an occasion, when I was an active priest, when at the seaside, late at night — and alone — a father and mother with their sobbing child stopped me.

"Father," they said, "our child is in agony with neuralgia — we can't do anything for her! Will you give her your blessing?"

I blessed the little girl and touched her cheek.

At once her sobs ceased. "Oh Mother," she said, "I'm all right — the pain's gone!"

When the great epidemic of flu was causing havoc in the west of Ireland, I was called one day to visit a fine young man who was dying. The flu was so bad, so virulent at the time, that to be stricken meant to die. But I was a priest and I had power from God. I visited the lad, prayed with him and for him, and gave him a special blessing. A few days later he was up and well.

Every priest knows of these coincidences and few priests but know more of them than I.

When we believe in God's benevolence and in His omnipresence it is reasonable for us to see the hand of God in things that happen. We see the hand of God dramatically active in the little spiritual experiences that are ours. Those lights that are ours; those illuminations that help us to understand the hitherto incomprehensible. Of a sudden we come across a spiritual treasure, an insight into a text of scripture that is of immense assistance to us. The text in its full meaning may be evident to others, but to us it has no significance. Then a light is ours and we see. We now can see so much!

I am asking in this chapter, and I think the meaning of the question is plain: "When is a miracle?" In order not to be evasive I am going to submit three occurrences belonging to the last year or two. As regards the outcome in each of the cases, I ask, was it due to coincidence and mere chance, or was it due to other causes? I pick these occurrences out of a host of others because, as I think, St. Anthony of Padua helped me out in one, and my Little Mother in the others. The fact that the substance or material involved in each happening was of relatively minor importance, does not, I think, affect the issue.

Occurrence number one:

The main road of Soquel, where I live, is broad and busy; day by day it grows busier, and cars rush through at much too fast a rate. It was windy this morning when I parked my car at the side of the road opposite the Post Office, where I collect my mail. As often happened I had to wait a while before being able to cross in safety.

There was a letter for me in a strange hand, and when I returned to my car I tore open the envelope to glance inside. In doing so I inadvertently tore off a bit of the corner where the sender's address was written. The scrap was about the size of a nickel and I dropped it out the window, where it was blown away. I was in a hurry and did not read the letter until I had an opportunity to do so in Santa Cruz, five miles away, an hour later.

The letter was from a young man who had read a book I wrote twenty-five years ago, criticizing the Jesuit Order. He had, the writer told me, intended to become a Jesuit, but, as a result of reading my book, he had abandoned the idea. Also, he added, my book had had the effect of shaking his faith! Now, he wanted to know if I still held the views I expressed in my book, or had I, perhaps, modified them? Did I still think badly of the Jesuit Order? Was I still critical of the Church?

Naturally, the letter disturbed me deeply. I resolved to answer it at once. It was plainly up to me, my serious duty, to disabuse the young man of my misleading teachings. I felt an urgent need to undo the harm I had done by my bitter, jaundiced, and unfair writings.

I glanced at the beginning of the letter to check up on the writer's address. To my surprise there was no address there. Then I turned to the envelope, only to find with deep dismay that I had mutilated the part of the envelope where it had been written. By throwing away the scrap of paper that I had torn off, I rendered it impossible to reply to the letter!

Then I thought that there might be a chance, one chance in a million, of recovering the missing scrap. I started my car and drove back as swiftly as I could, from Santa Cruz to Soquel, and parked as near as I could to the place where I had parked that morning. Meanwhile I turned to St. Anthony, fervently imploring his help. He, my mother's friend, would surely not fail me. And I asked that other marvelous friend of mine, St. Michael, to assist.

I began my hopeless search. The wind had blown papers hither and thither. The cars whirled by in numbers as I groped in the debris. I pounced on one likely scrap only to find it was part of a cigarette paper. I seized another scrap; it was part of an envelope but not my envelope. Then suddenly my eye fell on a tiny bit of white, and I felt no surprise. I knew I was not alone, unaided. On the bit I now picked up I found the missing part of the address I needed so badly. St. Anthony had befriended me — and St. Michael!

But had they? Was my little miracle only a coincidence? Was there nothing at all but mere chance at work in my experience?

Occurrence number two:

There is a long, narrow, and steep avenue leading down from this hilltop where I live to the Gulch road below. In particular, the last forty yards of it are steep and narrow, and they hang dangerously over the public road beneath. The avenue needed to be oiled and on one August 20 it was freshly and abundantly oiled with the thickest stuff I had ever seen. But I was told by the contractor that it would dry quickly and be usable and safe in a day or so.

August 22 is, of course, the feast of Mary's Immaculate Heart, and this year, of which I speak, it fell on a Sunday. My little Mother has always been good to me on this particular feast; every year there is a happy incident on this day, which I do not attribute to chance, but to her goodness. Furthermore, among the Sisters, dedicated to work all their lives in honor of Mary's sinless heart, I have a few good friends. One of these had written me that she was going to pray very specially for me on the coming feast of the Congregation.

There is an old proverb which says, "Few people are fit to be entrusted with themselves." I think Mary knows that very well, and takes account of it. Anyhow it is better to place oneself under her care.

Came Sunday morning, and at 7:40 a.m. I started my car to be in good time for early Mass. Early Mass on my little Mother's feast day! I noticed as soon as I started down the avenue that the oil was far from dry, but I drove very carefully and very slowly. I made it safely until I reached the last stretch, the last forty yards that overhung the road below. There the avenue was only nine feet wide, and terribly steep. And there the worst began to happen!

The car began to slide, and then to twist slowly. I had no longer any control whatever. The car was swinging around and it had to topple over on the road beneath. There was no more than a foot or two now between me and eternity. By all laws of physics and rules of gravity, as far as I could understand, the car was going over!

Of course, there was something besides physics and gravity — there were fervent eyes fixed upon Mary and fervent hearts praying for me. There was a tug at my little Mother's heart. When all seemed over the car, amazingly, began to steady itself and straighten out. Without my doing a thing, I found it back in the very middle of the avenue, and gently and correctly approaching the gate and passing quietly through.

What had happened? Had some other hand taken care of the unruly wheel? Or was it just another coincidence, a something due to mere chance?

Well, I'll say what I was going to say: "Thanks, little Mother, all the same!"

Occurrence number three:

There is a nun in Pennsylvania to whom I write on occasion, usually at Christmas and Easter. She is a deeply spiritual religious and a distinguished educator. Since the time when as a girl she visited the Italian shrine of Our Lady of Good Counsel, she has had a great devotion to our Lady under that title. This year, as the feast of Our Lady of Good Counsel approached, she had a great favor to obtain. She wanted our Lady to signify her approval of a spiritual project she had in mind. She asked in her great faith and simplicity that Our Lady of Good Counsel should give her a definite sign on her feast day, and that the sign should be three roses.

It was in total ignorance, not only of the spiritual project of my friend but also of the date of the feast of Our Lady of Good Counsel, that something prompted me to write to her. My letter, to Pennsylvania, went by ordinary mail, so I could not be at all sure of the time of delivery. In my letter, among other things, I told her how wonderful my roses were this year, and how I was able to keep, continuously, three lovely fresh roses before my little statue of Lourdes.

Was it not strange — or was it? — that my letter reached my friend on the morning of the feast of Our Lady of Good Counsel? Could it possibly be that our Lady was answering the good nun's prayer, and, at the same time, telling me that she liked my little gift to her?

CHAPTER VI

MY LITTLE MOTHER

MY LITTLE Mother has many pretty names. She is called *Porta Coeli* (Door of Heaven), *Fenestra Coeli* (Window of Heaven), and she is called the Second Eve. With the first Eve, "great Adam's wife," the second Eve shares in the mystery of mysteries, the joy of joys. But for the sin, the *felix culpa,* of the first Eve, Christ would never have come among us; and but for the *fiat,* the consent of the second Eve, we would be without the same divine Saviour.

The early Irish monks had a lively interest in and a moving understanding of the first Eve. We find in a tenth-century poem:

> I am Eve, great Adam's wife;
> 'Tis I that outraged Jesus of old;
> 'Tis I that robbed my children of heaven:
> By right, 'tis I that should have gone upon the cross.

In a poem, "Eve's Lament," belonging to the period, a poet-monk laid bare her soul in a striking picture:

> I had a kingly house to please me;
> Grievous the evil choice that disgraced me;
> Grievous the wicked advice that withered me;
> Alas! my hand is not pure.

'Tis I that plucked the apple,
Which went across my gullet;
So long as they endure in the light of day,
So long women will not cease from folly.

Full and poignant are Eve's reflections on the effects,
temporal and eternal, of her sin:

There would be no ice in any place;
There would be no glistening, windy winter;
There would be no hell; there would be no sorrow,
There would be no fear, if it were not for me.

The first Eve was a perfect creature, a reflection of
heavenly goodness and beauty, until her fall. Thereafter,
she was powerless to undo the evil she brought about.
Even had she "gone upon the cross" it would have been
of no avail. Her expiation of sin would have been insufficient. The curse she and Adam brought upon us all
could only be fully undone by Christ's redemption, in
which Mary, the second Eve, played the part of
co-redemptress.

Eve, our first mother, did us cruel wrong and suffered
for it. The second Eve, our true mother, undid that
wrong by giving us Jesus Christ. In giving Him to us
she gave us everything that is good. To this day, all that
is good comes to us through her hands. And Pius XII
tells us, quoting St. Bernard: "It is the will of God that
we should have nothing which has not passed through
the hands of Mary. . . . Such is the will of God, who
would have us obtain everything through the hands of
Mary."

Head of the human race, co-redemptress, mediatrix between God and us, mistress and queen of heaven; who but is stunned by the thought of Mary's greatness and her power? And who but is glad to know that tugging at her heart, all the time, in spite of her greatness, her love for us, her children?

"Every schoolboy knows," as the historian Macaulay would have said, that in loving Mary and in honoring her one loves and honors Christ. St. Bernard, the last of the Fathers, as Father Merton tells, "saw that the love of Jesus and Mary are so inseparable as to be the same. We cannot love Him without at the same time loving her, and our only reason for loving her is that we may love Him better."*

We can do nothing, nothing at all, without Mary. Without her we cannot come to Christ or linger close to Him. It is she who forms the image of Christ within us. It is she who gardens, cultivates, and nurtures our spiritual life, urging us incessantly to do "whatsoever He shall say" — above all to obey His: "Come to Me!"

I cannot but feel tenderly about my little Mother when I think of the deep love she has for me and for all her children, and like others I indulge in many a pious fancy. There is one such fancy that recurs, and I do not feel ashamed to reveal it.

As it unfolds, I see that supremely happy morning of Christ's resurrection. It is the break of dawn. Mary

---

* "The Last of the Fathers," by T. Merton, Harcourt, Brace & Co., 1954, p. 88.

is standing at the entrance of her dwelling, waiting, expectant. As her serene eyes reflect the first glimmer of the newborn light from the East, Christ is suddenly by her side. The gladdest moment of her existence is upon her. Her Son, in all the radiant beauty of His humanity, is with her again!

They are together and alone, but not for long! There is a knock, and knowing that I will be welcome, even at such a sacred, exclusive moment, I come in. Now, what happens? Who will be the first to speak to me? My Brother, my divine Friend? Or my Mother, my little Mother? Who will be first to welcome me? In my pious fancy I see Mary, without any surprise in her eyes, but only tender love, stretch out her arms to embrace me. Then, without knowing how it happened, I find myself at Jesus' feet, adoring Him, my God.

There are, as we know, righteous, God-fearing Christians who disapprove the way the Catholic Church presents the Christian faith to the world. The essence of their complaint is that Catholics make too much of Mary. Certainly Catholic doctrine is redolent of the glories of Mary: her Motherhood, her Virginity, her Immaculate Conception, her Assumption into heaven, her role as Co-redemptress, her exalted place as Queen and Mistress of heaven and earth. In the prayers of the Church no praise is too great for her. "Show me thy face, let thy voice sound in my ears, for thy voice is sweet and thy face comely. . . . All fair art thou, Mary, and the stain of original sin is not in thee. Happy art thou, Virgin Mary, and most worthy of all praise, who with thy virgin foot crushed the serpent's head. . . . Hail full of grace, the Lord is with thee, blessed art thou amongst women" (Mass of the Apparition of Lourdes).

I cannot here resist an impulse to quote a passage from a sermon on the Queenship of Mary, by the Apostolic Delegate, Most Rev. Amleto G. Cicognani, D.D. (Nov., 1954). This passage puts, in a grand way, the thought of every poor Catholic, from Tierra del Fuego to the Aran Isles. "What other woman on earth has been more celebrated, loved, venerated, invoked? To what other woman have been dedicated so many monuments, churches, chapels, shrines, sanctuaries; some so glorious as Loreto, Lourdes, Fatima? Innumerable cities, mountains and rivers, institutes and associations have derived their name from Mary. She has received affectionate, majestic, and genial homage from literature, oratory, poetry, sculpture, painting, music. No queen or empress has conquered hearts as Mary, truly the 'Conquistadora.'"

Once, on a Christmas eve, I was sitting before an open fire of blazing logs with a young scientist who took a dim view of Catholic doctrine. For him facts, or what he accepted as facts, were everything. And he did not admit that facts underlay the faith. As we sat, watching the fire, his eyes began to wander over a long line of Christmas cards, arranged on the mantelpiece above him. There were a hundred and fifty of them.

"You like facts?" I asked him, noticing his interest in the cards. "I do indeed!" he said.

I knew he still had in mind our discussion of religion. "We believers like them too," I told him, "and now you are looking at one. It's two thousand years since Mary, then a young, unknown Jewish maid, said: 'All generations shall call me blessed.' And there's no doubt about her making that prophecy. It's written down in innumerable codices of the earliest times.

"Now, look at those Christmas cards — they come from half a dozen lands that were unheard of in Mary's day, and eighty per cent of them glorify her. There you have a fact, hard as any fact can be, the fulfillment of an extraordinary prophecy. How can you account for that?"

I think my young friend was impressed. He made no effort at rebuttal. I hope the thought sank in.

The worship of Mary is no superfluity; no mere adjunct of Christian faith. It belongs as an essential. Were it not so, were it only a trimming of the faith, the Catholic priest who quits his duty and escapes into the wilderness would quickly discard it. He would soon forget about Mary. But this does not happen. In spite of his rebellion, his confusion of mind, his human faults, he clings to his faith and his hope in Mary. He trusts that she will somehow save him. And when moments of sorrow strike, and he sheds bitter tears over his fate, it is at the feet of his little Mother that he sheds those tears.

Of late I had occasion to write to another shepherd

without sheep who lives, lonely and poor, in an old shack in Florida. I wrote to beg his generous heart to spend itself in prayers for a fellow Dubliner, Tom, a "wandering priest" who had come to see me. I quote in part the reply I received from Florida.

My Dearest Boyd,

I shall ask our Blessed Mother to ask her divine Son to please look after the Dublin lad, Tom, whom you have been helping. For quite some time now, when anyone asks me to pray for him, invariably I ask her to pray for the person because *I know* she can, so much better than I can. . . . Stick and stick till death! Just so we can save our souls! Mary shall see to that, I am sure. . . . May we meet in heaven.

(*signed*) Bob

From another shepherd without sheep, who dwells in San Francisco, came the following letter, a few months ago. In it, he refers to a woodland shrine that he built as a boy in a tree stump. He coined the name *Stella Silvae* (Star of the Wood) for his Madonna.

Dear Boyd

This morning when I served Holy Mass in St. Ignatius Church, I offered this Mass and Holy Communion for you in thanksgiving to God for all He and you have done for me.

I beg the Blessed Virgin to chain you and me permanently to the tree stump of my devotion as her permanent slaves. I ask not for spiritual comfort but for grace to grow in spirituality: to grow in love of God and my fellow man.

Yours in Christ,
(*signed*) Paul

For seventy years I have known and loved Mary, though there was a long dark period, a score of years, when my love was weak and no spark at all in it. Many a million times I've asked Mary to help me in my last hour, and it is no small comfort to me to know, for certain, that she will do just that.

Back where memory begins, I see myself lighting an old-fashioned oil lamp before her statue in my little bedroom. It was a sweet statue of her and I knelt there as often as a thrush sings. And sometimes I had flowers for her, that my mother gave me from her garden; heliotrope, or geraniums, or red passionflower, or maybe a bright yellow rose.

Now, at the end of the day, I have another little statue in my room, the Immaculate of Lourdes. There are roses before it, almost all the year round, the loveliest roses, fresh and fair, for they never fail me on this hill. Now, with a kind of trusting pride, I can say to my little Mother: "Listen, Lady! I'm the old man who gives you flowers!"

Chapter VII

FAITH ON TRIAL

WE DISCOVER the goodness of Christ and we love Him. We possess Him by faith. We touch Him; we cling to Him; and we enjoy great peace. We begin to identify ourselves with Him, loving what He loves, wanting what He wants, always taking His side. "We put on Christ," making the imitation of Him the purpose of our life. We say, as did St. Paul: "I live now, not I, but Christ liveth in me." At last we have Christ within us, besides us. We know it; we feel it; and all is well with us — for a time!

Then there comes a strange, bewildering change. A darkness settles over us; the spiritual light we had goes out. We can no longer see or find Christ as we did. Our prayers sound hollow, and there is little comfort in them. The tabernacle takes on the appearance of an impregnable fortress: its strong door locks us out. The hand that we reach out seems unable to contact the hand of Christ. Where has He gone? Why has He left us?

To increase our misery temptations assail us and, deprived as its seems of Christ's strength, we fall into sin. The sin may not be great but it has all the ugliness and malice of sin. Weak and friendless, we are easy prey to the impulses of nature. Brightness and peace of soul are replaced by gloom. We are back again where we started, at the foot of the hill, and we have, as we think, forfeited all the gains of our gallant climb.

To lose Christ is a grievous calamity, the cause of utter sorrow and anguish — even if it be for only "three days." Mary and Joseph felt that sorrow, that sudden, unexpected catastrophe. One moment Jesus was with them; they heard Him and they saw Him; then He was gone entirely out of their lives. Theirs it was then to do what a hundred million lovers of Christ have had to do since: "to seek Christ sorrowing."

Mary's question to Christ, when at length she and Joseph found Him, was a question of astonished surprise: "Why hast Thou done so to us?" They had been good to Christ, always. They were the only two people in the whole world who knew Him and loved Him. Why, then, had He imposed this sorrow upon them? Why had He acted so heartlessly? Was it not hard on the part of the divine Boy to make his mother so lonely; to force tears into her gentle eyes? He explained — but neither she nor Joseph could understand.

When Christ disappears out of our lives, as He disappeared out of the lives of Mary and Joseph, it does not mean that He has ceased to be real, nor that He is tired of us and wants to be rid of us. He has some other motive for acting in the way He does; in that seemingly hard way. Spiritual teachers tell us that Christ leaves us in the darkness in order to try us — but that explanation is far from easy to understand.

When Christ leaves me, suddenly and inexplicably, I say to myself: "Well, He has left me, but I'm not going to leave Him. Now I am starting after Him, 'seeking Him in sorrow'; and I know He will let me find Him. And, when I find Him again, He will, as always in the past, be delighted!"

Faith in Christ is not realistic until one grasps that it entails pain as well as peace.

From the point of view of our human sensibilities Christ is "hard" at times. But would we wish Him to be otherwise? Often He refuses sympathy and comfort when we need it very badly. Often when we are hurt and depressed and lonely He will not say a single word to relieve us. He leaves us to sink and sicken in our misery. Well, what are we to say? I think we should say this: "Christ, You are my Christ! I love You as You are! I don't understand why You treat me so badly, but I love what You do and the way You do it!"

I look back on my life and see it as a long winding ascent up a steep hill. Christ is my guide and I follow Him as well as I can, but often I lose Him through my own fault, and often He simply leaves me to climb by myself. Here or there I overtake Him, and always our reunion is an intense joy, for I know He wants me to reach the top. But at some turn in the road, or due to some sin or mistake of mine, I lose Him again, and have to struggle alone for miles. Always up, up! And the top never comes into sight.

As the saying goes, "It's a great journey to the world's end"; but it's all the more difficult because the end remains unknown, a mystery. Christ, my guide, could tell me if He chose: "Only another mile or two! It's around yonder corner!" But He won't ever tell! He won't even encourage me by revealing to me that I will hold out.

And worse still, He makes the climb harder for me. He gives me things to carry, weak and exhausted though I be. The things He gives me to carry are not, of course, very heavy, but "in a long journey, even a straw weighs."

Of course, there are easy and happy stages in the ascent. At times, Christ shows that He does care — that He cares very much. He makes my heart glow with bright hope. But (alas! there is always a "but") He never goes so far as to say to me: "Take it easy now! You've made it!" And so, in fear and trembling, but withal in great hope, one has to go on climbing.

"Lord, I pray Thee," wrote a worn-out Jesuit scholar (Father Lessius), "draw my heart to Thee in the interior of my soul. There, far from the noise of the world, far from the importunate cares that overwhelm us, I would dwell near to Thee, to enjoy Thee, to love Thee, to venerate Thee, to hearken to Thy voice. To Thee will I recount the sorrows of my life of exile. There shall I find, near to Thee, the necessary consolations! Grant that I may never forget Thy presence within me. Oh! Thou light and sweetness of my soul! May I never forget

Thee! May the eyes of my soul always and everywhere be fixed on Thee."*

As we climb, Christ, as I have said, gives us something to carry; it may be sickness. Now we are sick, we have a pain, and our faith is on trial! The adage has it, "Sickness tells us what we are." At least it tells others, around us, what we are! If we were wise, most of us would go into hiding like animals, when we are sick, so as not to lose face. I think there must have been a chronic invalid in the family of the great Greek Euripides, for he wrote: "Better to be sick than tend the sick."

It is easy to write cynical or witty things about sick folk, but that is not my purpose here. My purpose is to analyze a little one of those very common trials of faith to which Christ's followers are subjected. Sickness is essentially such a trial, and one of its chief effects is to leave us virtually helpless; to make everything, even prayer, more difficult. We say, when sick: "I can't eat — I can't sleep — I can't work — I can't take an interest in anything!" Our bodies, that we are accustomed to rely on and to take care of, let us down. They let us down suddenly, and we do not know for how long. "Sickness comes on horseback and goes away on foot."

I remember visiting a saintly old priest who was gravely ill. He sat up in bed for a moment when I arrived. He shook hands with me, and then blurted out what was on his mind. He said something like

---

* *On the Divine Names.*

this: "Do your praying when you're well, Boyd! It's mighty hard to pray when you're sick!" Then he fell back on his pillow, gasping for breath. The old saint did not mean that it was impossible to pray when sick, but just that it was mighty hard to do so. He would not have admitted the truth of the saying: "The chamber of sickness is the chapel of devotion." He would, however, have seen in it the battleground of faith.

It's a long hard battle of faith, that the sick man or the sick woman has to fight. Each pain, each discomfort, has to be welcomed as a part of the holy will of God. Whether the pains and discomforts be great or little, they are nonetheless manifestations of God's wishes in our regard. Some are heroic in the way they bear pain; most of us are pretty cowardly. But, even though we be cowardly, we can still, in our faith, keep saying: "God wills it!"

Of sicknesses, the most inevitable and the most tedious is old age. And old age is never just that: it seldom comes alone. With this, I have no doubt, many of my readers will emphatically agree. What old man or old woman is there who has no complaint? And what old man or old woman is there whose faith is not on trial?

We, old people, all know full well that, unless we bless and love and thank God for our aches and pains and feeble sight and stiff joints, we can't enjoy the close companionship of Christ. We know that, just as we know that He does not love us less because our gums are toothless and our fingers are like claws.

For some of us the coming of old age is incredible. Personally I find it difficult to believe it. I still rub my eyes when I realize that I can no longer join in a rough game; sally out, alone, for a long swim; climb a ladder and walk across a sloping roof. Why can't I hurry uphill after Bran when he starts for a deer? Why can't I fling off my coat, when some kids are around, and say to them: "Come on! Let's go!"? Must I forever henceforward move shyly to a seat in the shade, away from noise and stir, a retiring old has-been?

Still harder do I find it not to take for granted the gay smile of the girl who sells me envelopes at Woolworth's, or of the lad who fills five octane into the tank of my car. Why do I feel thrilled and elated on receiving that gratuitous smile?

The fact is, I no longer expect young people to bother about being nice to me. That is too much for a dull, toothless old man to expect. The incredible has happened. Without my grasping it, a mighty change has overtaken me — an iron curtain of unnoticed winters has slipped down between me and the things that used to be mine in the past!

"Why doesn't he take vitamins? He'd feel O.K. if he took them!" The advice is good, the very best, if by vitamins is meant the "vitamin" that gives an old man new life: "the living Bread that gives life." Every old man who follows Christ depends upon It.

So our faith is on trial whenever Christ leaves us to fend for ourselves; or whenever He gives us a pain to carry; or when, at last, He bids us be content with shaky hands and uncertain feet. It is our faith in Him that Christ wants most. It is our faith that endears us to Him. "Without faith it is impossible to please God" (Hebr. 9:6). Faith, as St. Thomas taught, is our direct approach to Christ. (*Primus autem accessus ad Deum est per fidem.*) When our faith is on trial, if we are "strong in faith" (1 Pet. 5:9), we have our supreme opportunity of winning Christ's heart. How wonderful, how precious a possession is faith in Christ, that supreme gift of God!

If I may speak for old men, and especially for old priests who failed in their day, I say: "You may have your youth! You may have your buoyancy and élan! You may have your wealth, your power, and your genius, but give me faith! Give me the faith that gives me Christ, as my Companion, my Friend, my Brother! With Him there is no despair or helplessness in sickness, nor is there any shame or weakness in old age!"

Chapter VIII

REALISM IN FAITH

A CATHOLIC worshiper enters the chapel, genuflects, and kneels before the tabernacle. He is reverential in his demeanor, full of respect, edifying as can be. He reminds himself of the Divine Presence: he acts "as if" he were kneeling before Christ. But how far does he grasp the fact that he is kneeling before Christ, that the Man God sees him, hears him, welcomes him? Is he reacting simply, frankly, to the actuality of Christ's physical presence, or is there a lack of realism in his conduct?

There were in Belgium, when I studied at Louvain, two *Pères Petit*. They were, both of them, small of build; the smaller, a very simple, holy man, was called *petit Père Petit*. Rather than tell about him myself, I will use the words of Father Willie Doyle.

"There is a wonderful little old priest here (*petit Père Petit*), small in name and small in size — he is about three feet high. He is eighty-five but as active as a man of thirty, being constantly away giving retreats. I have tried several times getting down to the chapel at four in the morning before him, but he was always there when I came in. He is a dear, saintly old man with wonderful faith and simplicity. In the middle of an exhortation in the chapel, he will turn round to the tabernacle and say: 'Is not that true, my Jesus?' "*

That small episode will suggest what realism in faith means. Realism in faith is not the fruit of vivid imagining; nor is it the result of mental and emotional effort; it is the plain good sense of allowing faith to have its way; of not interfering with faith.

Father Petit belonged among the Walloons; the Flamands were still more simple and forthright. At this same time, the famous Father Arthur Vermeersch lived in the college where I was studying. I regard him also as an exemplar of saintly realism. He was a small, energetic man, with a deeply lined face, and eyes that always twinkled with a brave smile. He had been a lawyer before entering the Jesuit Order; and he was destined to be a great moralist and canonist.

He was a dynamo of energy, doing this and that at high speed; a miser of time, wearing chains and hair shirts, blasting his way through mountains of work; and then, of a sudden, at the call of obedience he could relax. And how realistically he relaxed: as though he heard Christ's whisper: "Now, Arthur, take it easy for a half hour!"

Once he gave me a picture of realism that I can never forget. It was a Thursday, toward the end of dinner, when, as usual, there was a glass of red wine for all. Father Vermeersch was not far from me, and

---

* *Father William Doyle, S.J.*, by Prof. Alfred O'Rahilly, Longmans, Green & Co., 1925, p. 57.

I saw him leaning back, resting against the refectory wall. His smile was there, as usual, and he was eyeing the empty glass in his hand. Then something caught his eye. There was still one little drop of wine in the bottom of his glass! Good Flamand that he was, he hated waste. He raised the glass and tilted it, until it was almost upside down: then out came his tongue to catch the missing drop — that last little spot of reality! He seemed to sigh as he replaced his glass on the table.

If a material thing was real for Father Vermeersch, still more was a spiritual thing, a spiritual task. The two minute visit he would make to the chapel, as he rushed from class to class, was like a short cyclone. He tore in for one hundred and twenty seconds of ecstasy; then out he dashed. It was an example of the Little Flower's expression: "an invisible hurricane of love."

There is no pretense, no make-believe, no hesitation in the act of faith of a realist. The quality of actuality is there. It has no hollow sound. The hand of Christ, that he holds by faith, is not a phantom hand. It is Christ's own hand, though it is not sensibly felt.

We must always bear in mind, of course, that faith is God's gift, a divine endowment. If it increases, grows stronger, becomes more realistic and factual, that, too, is due to God's giving. We can fancy a martyr, St. Lawrence for example, saying to himself (in modern language): "This is it!" when he had to face the torture of fire. But we would minimize the realism of St. Lawrence, if we did not also picture him as saying:

"This is it!" when a bell sounded to call him to offer Mass. "This is it!" is the habitual thought and conviction of the realist face to face with an inspiration of grace.

Once, when I was young, I heard a story in a retreat that has remained with me all my life. It was the story of a mountain climber who had gained the summit of an alpine peak but had never returned. His great ambition had been to make his way alone to the top. He had succeeded, but it was his end. Later, when his body was found on the summit, a note in his handwriting was found beside him. The note read: "It is very cold — and I see nothing." The application of this story, to the man whose faith is vague, hesitating, lifeless, is obvious. In the presence of Christ he is as one blindfolded. He cannot contact Christ or sense Christ's warmth. All he says is: "It is very cold — and I see nothing!"

The man whose faith is not real is naturally unhappy and very unsettled in mind. He finds himself immersed in material reality. About that he has no doubt. Also, he is not wholly deaf to the sounds of the spiritual world; the voice of conscience; the promptings of grace; but they are not very real for him. He is, in a way, uncertain about the spiritual life. He can't adjust himself to a straight, sure course of action. He has no true trust in faith! We must, if we are realists, trust our faith: trust it outright and forever.

But let me insert a word of caution. The faith in which we trust must be the reasoned, revealed, orthodox faith of the Church, and not any fancied scheme of things.

There are offshoots of piety that belong in no way to the faith: there are "voices" and "inspirations" that are not to be trusted, for they have not the hallmark of faith. It is not realism but foolishness to be insipidly credulous.

There is a story of an old Irishwoman at home who was well known for her unbalanced piety, and also for the fact that she was looking for a good price for an old donkey that she was tired of feeding. It was Christmas time, and there was a large crib in the parish church, with figures of the Madonna and the Infant Jesus. The old woman was kneeling, praying aloud, and a local playboy, who happened to be there, heard what she was saying and slipped behind the crib, unnoticed.

As her prayer went on, and she was asking our Lady to get her "a good price for her donkey," a seemingly childlike voice reached her ears, telling her: "You're expecting too much!"

The poor woman was startled for a moment. Then she exclaimed angrily: "Hush, Child! And let your holy Mother speak!"

One cannot have more faith than to make an act of faith; to be realistic in one's faith is to live by faith. One of the best of such acts is an act of love.

A letter comes from a poor fellow you know. The letter reveals distress and, perhaps, actual poverty. It's not a very tactful letter and it tends to disgust you. "Why can't he leave me alone!" you say. Then, from the unknown depths of your heart arise the words: "What

you do for the least of My little ones you do for Me!"
At once you search for your writing pad and checkbook,
and there is a kind note and a kind present on the way.
That is an act of faith in the garment of love: realistic
faith; realistic love. The more real our love of Christ
is, the more real will be our faith in Him.

A guest comes to your house: it is not only your
hospitality that is put to the test but also your faith.
Is your faith as realistic as the monk poet of old thought
it should be?

> Oh! King of Stars,
> Whether my house be dark or bright,
> Never shall it be closed against anyone,
> Lest Christ close His house against me!

> If there be a guest in your house,
> And you conceal aught from him.
>   'Tis not the guest that will be without it,
>   But Jesus, Mary's Son!

We are all aware that at times our faith is seemingly
very realistic. We feel — we know, that we are in close,
vivid, actual contact with Christ, and it makes us happy
to be in that state. Like the disciples walking with the
hidden Christ, to Emmaus, for an unaccountable reason
our "hearts burn." Alas! that the fire goes out so soon!

Our hearts burn, after Holy Communion, or after
a good confession, or just on a sudden, and unaccount-
ably, and at once we are realists in our faith. But that
is not enough. Our "maddening joy" is often short-lived.
Then come those dark hours, when everything materially

and spiritually goes wrong. Still our realism must be maintained. How can we attain that desirable, that necessary state?

If I tell how I, when God gives me the grace to do so, awaken (or rather rediscover) this realism it may help others to find a method for themselves.

For example, I find myself following a cow track through the fields. Bran is off in front, or around somewhere. I'm not anxious about him for I know he will take good care not to lose his master. I'm alone now and I'm praying . . . thinking about Christ . . . thinking like the eighth-century Irish monk:

> Thou my best thought, by day and by night,
> Waking or sleeping. Thy presence my light.

Then there comes up Christ's word: "Come to Me!" and I obey. Now, I am with Christ. At the back of my head there is the sure conviction that it is well for us always to do what He tells us to do; and further, that we please Him by doing what He tells us to do.

Next, I find Christ saying: "Reach hither your hand!" and I do just that. He does not mean that I should stand there with my hand out in the empty air. No! He tells me to give Him my hand so that it may rest in His hand. I am imagining nothing, improvising nothing: I'm just obeying His word — and that makes the whole situation very real for me. I'm not even interested in trying to picture Christ — only to be with Him.

Now, as I hold His hand, what am I to do? To make

a great effort of some kind in the direction of some state of spiritual sublimity? No! He didn't tell me to make any effort, but He said: "Be not afraid! Let not your heart be troubled! Rest a little!" As I walk, side by side, with Christ, I prefer to be resting. Of course, I take care, as we walk, that there be a clean, clear way for Him. I move accordingly, to give Him free way.

If, as he has done, the devil whispers in my ear: "This will make you spiritually proud! You'll think yourself a great fellow, henceforth!" I have my answer for the devil . . . or rather the answer that quiets my anxieties. All the while I am near Christ His grace is healing me of every fault, of every impulse of pride.

If any other worry crosses my mind, about the becomingness and good sense of this "walking with Christ," I remind myself that I am acting under obedience. Everything I'm doing Christ has told me to do. Why then should I be afraid of doing it, or of telling what I do? Thus I enter, for a time at least, into realistic faith, through the safe gateway of obedience. Whom did Christ address when He said: "I shall be with you always"? By *you*, he meant you — and He meant me. He is never far away — and that's the truth!

CHAPTER IX

CHRIST'S CHALLENGE

CHRIST stands alone, incomparable, on the high terrain of human history. He is seen by all; He cannot but be seen. He draws the eyes of all men to Himself. There are, to be sure, puppets in glamorous robes on that high terrain, who wave their arms and cry: "Look at me!" But the wise eye of mankind sees that they are only "men of straw," with feet of clay; it comes to rest on Christ.

Christ speaks and all can hear. His voice carries a challenge. It is not an angry, boastful challenge. It is sincere, modest, appealing. It is not inspired by contempt, or fear, or hate; but by love. He knows all men are thirsty for peace, for fulfillment, for happiness. He knows how unsettled their hearts are. He says: "If any man thirst let him come to me and drink" (Jn. 7:37). He puts His challenge in words, other words, that are still easier to understand: He says: "Come to Me! Come and see!"

When I write about Christ's challenge: "Come to Me! Come and see!" I know these words are addressed to me, as well as to you. Christ challenges us to find out about Him, by approaching Him and meeting Him. He says, in effect: "Do not be afraid to do so. It is not fair to judge of Me by hearsay. It is not fair to stand far off and judge me as a hostile witness, from a great distance. Come and drink with Me. Why are you afraid to learn about Me?"

The first ears that Christ's definite challenge reached were those of two fairly well-to-do fishermen of Galilee, Andrew and John. It happened that they were visiting with John the Baptist. Indeed, they were much attached to that great preacher; they were among his followers, his disciples. This day, as they talked with John, he suddenly turned and pointed to a young man who was passing and cried: "Behold the Lamb of God!" Astonished, they determined to find out more about this Young Man and they began to follow him.

Soon, He noticed that they were following and said: "What seek ye?" Andrew and John answered: "Master, where dwellest thou?" There followed Jesus' never dying challenge: "Come and see!" Then these two fishermen gave to all the world an example of common-sense conduct in respect to Jesus, that of finding out about Him.

Emerson once wrote: "Nothing astonishes men so much as common sense and plain dealing." Emerson had in mind common sense and plain dealing in respect to the ordinary affairs of life, and he found it astonishing. Needless to say, it is still more astonishing in respect to finding out about Christ. To the end of time men and women will be unable to abandon ridiculous misunderstandings of Christ because they won't visit Him and talk to Him.

But to return to Andrew and John. They continued after Jesus until He reached His little home or cabin. Then they sat down and listened to Him. "They stayed with Him that day" (Jn. 1:39).

Andrew and John liked Jesus. In His eyes there was no deception, but grace and truth. Like others, they found that "no one ever spoke like this man." Christ enlightened them and touched their hearts and they found they could not but believe in Him. Christ did not perform any miracle for them — they were not won over by legerdemain or put under hypnotic spell. They were plain, wide-awake, shrewd workmen — knowing what was what — and they believed!

After the interview was over, Andrew sought out his brother Peter, and said; "We have found the Messias, the Christ." He made Peter "come and see." "He brought him to Jesus."

Philip was soon won over by meeting Jesus, and he told his friend Nathaniel about Him. "Come and see!" he said to Nathaniel, using the words of Christ's challenge.

A great change took place in the world — history was made as soon as men began to find out about Christ, to accept His challenge with honesty.

There was another, after Andrew, who heard and answered Christ's challenge, though he did so in a timid, hesitating way. He was Nicodemus, "a ruler of the Jews." He came by night, fearing that he might be seen visiting Jesus. He said: "Rabbi, we know that Thou art come a teacher from God."

Jesus revealed to him the gist of His mission on earth, namely to teach mankind the need of a spiritual rebirth. "Men love darkness rather than light for their works are evil." Jesus told Nicodemus: "The light is come into the world." He told him: "Those who believe in Me will not perish!"

Nicodemus too, was won over by Christ. He found that "in God's light we see light" (Ps. 35).

The Gospels tell of many others, from Magdalen to the Good Thief, who in one way or other "came to see" Christ, and came to believe. Christ knocked at their hearts; they opened the door of their hearts; Christ entered.

It needed daring to accept Christ's challenge. It still needs daring: faith is for the brave, not for the cowardly and pusillanimous. The courage of the believer consists in accepting the forbidding possibility that the things we see and value are not what we esteemed them to be, but worthless; the possibility that unseen things, spiritual eternal things, alone are of worth. Who but the daring and the brave can say with St. Paul: "We look not at the things which are seen, but at the things which are not seen. For the things which are seen are temporal, but the things which are not seen are eternal" (2 Cor. 4:18).

How terrific is Christ's challenge! The unfrowning Christ looked into the eyes of men and said: "Your philosophy of life is a lie. Follow Me. I am the way, the truth, the life!"

If we let our memory roam over the life and works of Christ we see Him as the great triumphant Challenger of all things, of all powers, as He reveals His truth, His omnipotence, His divinity.

He challenged the powers of nature: He controlled the angry seas and the wind. He challenged disease: He gave back sight to the blind, and cleansed lepers. He challenged hitherto invincible death: He raised to life Jairus' daughter and His friend Lazarus. He challenged the law of nature and turned water into wine. He challenged the hate and revenge of the human heart and showed men the superiority of love and forgiveness. He challenged hypocrisy and lying. He challenged the worth of pride and showed the beauty of childlike humility. He challenged the wrath and wickedness of His enemies, and though they succeeded in crucifying Him, He rose again from the dead in triumph!

What think ye of the Christ? Who is like to Christ?

What I have said, thus far, about Christ's challenge is all in the open; written down for all men to read; the common knowledge of all mankind. But there is another Christ who issues challenges that are secret and addressed to the individual heart. This Christ is the "Hound of Heaven" who pursues this soul and that, whispering, beckoning, calling. This Christ is tireless, relentless, insatiable. He wants to take possession of your heart and of mine. He defies you and me to refuse Him!

It would be an easy matter to illustrate, from the

confessions of the great saints, Teresa of Avila, Ignatius of Loyola, Francis of Sales, and a hundred others, how Christ was forever challenging them to withhold any corner of their hearts from Him, or to refuse Him any but the most pure and perfect trust. He said to each of them in turn, whether in this century or that, in this land or another: "My Child, I defy you to refuse Me anything!" They knew and loved Him so much! He knew the love they had for Him.

But even among Christ's "little friends" we find the frank recognition of Christ's insatiable desire to possess the human heart in its entirety, His relentless insistence: "Do this or that for Me! I defy you to refuse!"

Among these "little friends" there was one I knew well; under whose authority I lived at school — Father Willie Doyle. After his heroic, sacrificial death on the battlefield, his spiritual notes were published.* A few extracts from these notes will exemplify what I mean when I speak of Christ as a hidden Challenger of the human heart.

Ten years before his death, in 1917, Father Willie wrote, apropos of a retreat: "He has been tugging at my heart for so many years, urging me in so many ways to give myself wholly to Him, to give all and refuse Him nothing."

Later, we read: "I am more and more convinced that Jesus is asking from me the complete and absolute sacri-

---

* See reference on page 57 above.

fice of every gratification, pleasure, self-indulgence, and comfort which, within the Rule, and without injuring my health and work, I can give Him."

Again: "Even walking along the streets I feel God tugging at my heart . . . urging, urging, urging me to give myself up absolutely to Him and to His service."

How did Father Willie respond to these challenges of Christ for wholehearted self-sacrifice and self-denial? Here is one example of his responses — it may read strangely to some eyes; others will understand.

At the time he was strenuously engaged in giving a mission in Glasgow, Scotland, and he was suffering from a cold. But, all the same, at night, he made his way unobserved to the church. Then: "I made the Holy Hour prostrate on the marble flags, and by moving from time to time I continued to get the full benefit of the cold. Then for two hours I made the Stations of the Cross, standing, kneeling, and prostrate, taking fourteen strokes of the discipline at each Station. For the rest of the night I remained kneeling before the tabernacle, at intervals with arms outstretched, till I could bear the agony of this no longer."

And Willie Doyle was no morbid type, but gay, playful, full of pranks, and always ready to oblige. At the front (France, 1917), the soldiers and officers alike loved him for his joyous courage and kindness and — broadmindedness!

Christ's "little friends" by the thousands today hear His challenging voice in their ears. So it will be until the end of time, for He is the same Christ "yesterday, today, forever." He will not leave them alone. He loves them too much to do so.

Among the friends I have, whom I love and value dearly, there are some students of science, bright minds, young men of charm, wit, and zest. But, for some of them at least, science, knowledge is everything; Christ is only a vague, far-off, unreal figure on the horizon of uncertain interests.

How can I tell them that Christ is not vague or far-off or unreal? How can I persuade them to "come and see" Him and to "reach out their hands" to Him as He asks? How can I get it into their heads that science and knowledge lack meaning unless shot through with faith?

I know, for myself, that if all the discoveries of science were unloaded into my brain — and if, *per impossibile,* there were added to that great heap discoveries yet to be made by the inquisitive minds of researchers for the next thousand years to come — my brain would still be dark, restless, wistful, until I had learned and accepted the truth that Christ imparts — the truth about spiritual life — the truth of life everlasting.

Let men heap up learning until it reaches the stature of Mount Olympus, but it still remains heavily dark until faith inspires understanding. "Unless you believe you will not understand" (St. Augustine).

CHAPTER X

WANTED — A FRIEND

ON THE door of the old place where a shepherd without sheep lives in his loneliness, there hangs a notice: "Wanted — A Friend." His loneliness, if that is the right word for his state, is inevitable and incurable. It can't be helped.

The priesthood changes a man — forever. It is only as an active priest that he fits in, that he belongs. Once he removes from that state, or once he is removed, he becomes (I have no other expression than the familiar one) "a fish out of water." In no respect whatever is he like other men, and he knows it.

He meets a priest who *knows;* the priest is a bit too cordial, too warm in his greeting. He meets a nun who *knows;* and the nun is a bit too kind, too charitable, too anxious to say the exactly right thing. He meets a good lay Catholic who *knows;* and the lay Catholic is too grimly respectful. Should it be his lot to meet a bishop, His Excellency overwhelms him with pastoral paternity. Priest, nun, layman, all do their best to adopt the right attitude toward a repentant shepherd, but it is beyond their tact and insight to succeed. I wish I had a delicate, skillful pen to analyze this strange impossibility of normalcy between the faithful one and the unfaithful.

I said impossibility. But there was one, a young "wild Irish" curate from Limerick, for whom it wasn't impossible to be normal with me. Father Kevin would, any time he was passing near, break into my house, drive my dog into a delirium of excitement, and start yelling for a cup of Irish tea! Then he'd yarn! But Father Kevin was called to another parish, and there was no one to take his place.

Perhaps we are too sensitive, and do not realize that fact. We should not resent it, when other folk put on their moral Sunday best when talking to us. We are oddities, of course; but we should try to forget it.

In respect of letters, things are different. The nicest and most agreeable letters are written to us; letters such as we might receive were we active and in uniform. But letters do not satisfy the yearning there is in a silenced priest's heart for the kind of friendships he knew in the old days.

"Wanted — A Friend." The stray shepherd reads his own sign, that expression of his heart. As he dwells on it he understands better the meaning of Christ: the great thing that Christ offers. He finds that his loneliness is throwing him into the arms of Christ — it is a blessed loneliness. Now he has no choice but to accept the despised friendship of Christ and to find out for himself that man is mad and evil, in despising such wonderful friendship.

He recalls that Christ has taken the initiative; has already given him the name friend — "I call you friend";

and has first begun to love. St. Teresa of Avila used to say: "Love draws forth love." Are we not already loving Christ before we know it? Are we not, in so doing, unconsciously responding to His love?

We wonder, of course, how or why it can be that Christ wants our friendship and our love. Not being theologians we do not attempt to formulate the right answer. We just accept the fact that it is so — while still wondering. What He wants He is ready to purchase; and He purchases our friendship in the only way it can be purchased, by giving us His friendship. "Friendship," says the proverb, "is purchased by friendship." How much we measure out to Christ, in return for what He pays, is up to us.

If I ask the question: "Is Christ a good Friend to me?" I ask it only to keep my mind busy thinking about Him, thinking of all the hundred and one gifts He has given me, during seventy years gone by. I ask: "Has He ever, once, done me any harm?" and I have to answer: "Never!" Always He sought my good, and the good of those I dearly loved. So, I call my Friend, Christ, a good Friend, for I believe in the old proverb: "He is a good friend that doth thee good!"

I have said, more than once, I think, that I do not know and cannot foresee into what hands this book may fall. Therefore, I have to consider the possibility of its falling into the hands of people of little or no faith, who will say: "How absurd! How preposterous! How could a God and a human be friends? Friendship presupposes equality. What equality exists between that fellow and God?"

Well, for me, the question of equality between the God-Man, Christ, and myself is a mystery but not a difficulty. Through Christ's redemption, I became the son of God the Father, by adoption. I am God's son, and Christ's brother; His brother by adoption and by grace. By adoption, too, I am the son of Mary, Christ's mother. And so, there is equality between us; there is the perfect basis of friendship.

But, there seems to be another difficulty (that an unbeliever would not think of), a real difficulty against the possibility of real friendship between Christ and me. This difficulty is pinpointed by the adage, "Without confidence there is no friendship." And the confidence must be mutual.

Obviously there is no difficulty in my having confidence in Christ; that is the easiest thing in the whole world! But how can Christ have confidence in me? How can he have any confidence whatever in me? I have failed Him, betrayed Him, not once or twice, but a thousand times. I have sworn in the most solemn manner to the most solemn vows, only to abandon them. How can He render me that trust that is indispensable in friendship?

I know there is an answer to this difficulty that worries and frightens me, but I do not know what it is. I think it may lie in the fact that Christ substitutes His will to save me, and to keep me in His love, for my capacity to remain faithful. The answer may lie in those divine words of His anent His friends: "No one shall snatch them from My grasp!"

It may be queer, now, to quote a line from an old pagan, Aristotle, and apply it to my discussion of friendship with Christ. But it was a wise saying that he uttered: "Many a friendship is lost through lack of speaking!"

Christ is around! He is near! How can we help but speak to Him; ask Him questions; tell Him things; enjoy silent intercourse with Him? He has said, and says again each day more intimately, so many things to us, that it is our part to answer Him, to discuss with Him what He says.

"Come to Me," He says.

I answer: "Here I am, Master! Now that I've done what You asked, let me rest with You!"

"My Child, give Me your heart!" He says, another time.

And I reply, "Master, I've already given You my heart, but not all of it. I'm still a bit afraid to do that. You haven't yet given me the grace to surrender myself completely to You. You'll have to take my heart Yourself, in Your own way, if You must have it completely!"

We have to keep on talking and walking with Christ, in an intimate way and unafraid, unless we are to face the dreadful loss of His friendship. It is said: "Friendship stands not on one side." Let's talk back, affectionately, to Christ when He talks to us. It's easy as that!

A friend of Christ takes up his (or her) pen to write and soon the one (and only) story that he (or she) knows begins to unfold. It's the story of his (or her) Friend, Christ. It's a great proof of faith, this firsthand account of the one and only celebrity that is really news-worthy — Christ. And each *raconteur* displays the ingenuous vanity of John, the Evangelist, in the ever recurring claim and boast: "I am the disciple whom Jesus loved!" How can they all, from John of the Cross to Thomas More, from Brigid of Kildare to Thérèse of Liseux, make the same claim, and each one truthfully? Well, we are all of us, in a sense, first in Christ's love, because we are all uniquely different in His eyes.

"Wanted — A Friend." But the poor man who lives here is a beggar. Christ knocks and comes in. He says: "Love is love in beggar and king." So He is satisfied to have the love that a beggar gives.

"Wanted — A Friend." But the man who lives here is a miser; he never gives anyone credit. Christ knocks and comes in. He says: "You already have My love. Love those who love thee. I do not require credit." So even the meanest, most suspicious soul may safely take Christ for Friend.

"Wanted — A Friend." But the poor man who lives here alone is a coward, a miserable frightened creature. Christ knocks and comes in. He smiles, and says: "Be not afraid! I know that love requires daring, but I will give you that daring." So even a craven coward may securely take Christ as his Friend.

Sunday mornings, at Mass, I let my eyes rest a moment on the people, men or women, who are old and feeble; on the disabled ones, if any; on those who look less well dressed; on those men or women who are awkward and unattractive; and I think of Christ's happiness that they are there, near Him. He loves them all.

And when Communion time comes, I watch with nostalgia in my heart the priest in vestments carrying the Living Bread that is Christ to eager lips. It makes me happy to see that faith that is love; and that love that is faith. He who loves, believes!

My time comes to receive Christ, when the last railful is all but spent. I know, so well, that Christ will not overlook me. "The poor have no friends," you say? That's not how Christ looks on things! That's not His way!

Dear Master and Friend! It is a great comfort for me to have You — to be able to come to You; and talk to You; and rest with You! I don't know what I would or could do without You! How could I face what remains of my life, and my death that awaits me, without You?

You are my God, and my All; my Consolation, and my Salvation! I love You! I trust in You! I believe with my whole soul and mind and heart in You! But I beg You to increase my love, my trust, my faith in You — and to increase my love, my trust, and my faith in Your Mother and mine, in Mary! Jesus, as I write I am touching You, and Your grace is pouring into my soul and healing me. You are creating Your divine image in me and making me like to You! That is Your way, and always I love what You do, and the manner in which You act! My Friend! Stay with me always, dwelling in my heart!

Chapter XI

THE GOOD FIGHT

IN THE mind of a priest in hiding there hover nostalgic memories and the faces of great and good pastors who were faithful to the end. Foremost among these faces is that of the Curé d'Ars, St. John Mary Vianney (1786–1859), who might well be called "the priest's saint." From his lips seem to come with persuasive insistence Paul's words to Timothy: "Fight the good fight of faith" (1 Tim. 6:12).

St. John Vianney is the exemplar of the faithful priest, the shepherd who watches and works and does not stray from his sheep.

I can only guess why it makes me proud and happy to think about the grand old priest who "stuck it out" to the end. Maybe in my admiration I relive, vicariously, what might have been. Also, I confess to a feeling of being confused, as would happen were one to see the same person, here, there, and everywhere. I mean that the Curé of Ars was not just one kind old nineteenth-century French pastor, but he reappears in every other parish throughout the Catholic world, to the joy and the glory of the Church.

He was, for instance, my parish priest near Dublin

when I was a child. He was the tall, austere, prayerful Archdeacon Walsh, who lived for and in his parish, built its splendid granite church and towering steeple. The steeple was his pride, the only pride he indulged in. I see him still, after his early Mass, standing outside the church, craning his neck and tilting back his head, to look where it met the sky.

The Curé of Ars means much to us all and is easily loved, because in the course of our wanderings we have known him, seen him help the poor, hasten to sick calls, listen kindly and patiently to our sins, and "carry on" even in utter feebleness, the work he began for Christ.

As a lad, a farm boy with little education, but a great longing to be a priest, John Vianney had difficulties. He couldn't make head or tail of Latin grammar, but in time (1812) he was ordained; and three years later, when France's Little Corporal hastened, in defeat, from Waterloo (June, 1815), Christ's Little Corporal began as Curé of Ars a series of spiritual victories, the good effects of which last until today.

The Curé of Ars believed in Christ with a strong, simple, serene faith. His faith was the secret of his wonderful success. For the forty-seven years of his uninterrupted service his faith grew, and day by day Christ became more visible in him. He was so like to Christ, so truly Christ, that "publicans and sinners drew near to hear him" (Lk. 15:1). The hundreds of thousands who came to Ars to see and hear and touch him found Christ's virtue "coming out of him." He forgave, advised, comforted, and read men's hearts. Like Christ, "He knew what was in man" (Jn. 2:25). The zeal, prayer, and penance that the Church saw in him did not, strangely, repel men but attracted them. He was another "lovable saint," that ever-recurring, baffling phenomenon of a sinful world that hates virtue.

No picture, even by the greatest of the great masters, was so true and good a portrait of Christ as was this gentle, affable old Curé. But what is there to wonder at in that? Is not Christ able to paint? And is it not Christ who painted this picture of Himself, the Curé of Ars? And could it not be that the brush that Christ used to paint His self-portrait was the teeming, fine-fibered faith of His parish priest?

"Old John," as I presume his local brother Curés called him, would have said of himself: "I'm only a poor, sinful priest, trying to do the best I can, and that's not much." He would not have told of his long days spent in hearing confessions, visiting the sick, instructing the ignorant, caring for orphans, begging bread for the hungry. He would not have told of sixteen to eighteen hours work in the day, nor of his indifference to food and sleep. Nor would he have groaned: "Forty-seven years is too long a spell!"

Some may praise most of all the charity of the Curé of Ars; others his miracles; others again his penance and his prayers. But for me his great, immortal glory is the faith in him that made possible — and, in a way, easy — his tremendous work. His faith, as I have said, was forty-seven years agrowing. It was a wondrous big and beautiful tree by the day it dissolved into the Vision of God.

The Curé had been a loyal and faithful friend of Christ. To be Christ's good friend is man's highest dignity.

As a young man, when I read about the French revolutionary era, I conceived a great enthusiasm for Napoleon Bonaparte. I read all that I could find about him and I selected him as one of the greatest geniuses and heroes of all times. I wrote and lectured on him, and, with his gallant veterans, I gloried in his victories and wept over his defeats.

About the Curé of Ars, who witnessed at close quarters Napoleon's rise and fall, I knew nothing. There was no mention of him in popular books of history. He was too humble, too commonplace a person for historians to write about. Royal palaces shook to the cry: *"Vive L'Empereur!"* — but who, save tramps, would say more than *"Bonjour, mon Père!"* to the Curé of Ars?

But faith in Christ sinks into a man's mind and changes his outlook and clarifies his thoughts. Now I see the great Napoleon in a different light; not as a hero, but as a vainglorious cock of the walk. I see, with Byron, "the gloom of his glory," and grieve that he left France, stricken and "sunk in her worth."

Of the two men, the Curé and the General, who contributed most to France's progress?

There is a dark, bitter saying of R. G. Ingersoll: "The history of progress is written in the lives of infidels." Napoleon, who though not a formal unbeliever, stood for the cause of infidels, wrought the ruin and enslavery of his race. Was that progress? The Curé of Ars, the man of faith, spent his every hour in building for human happiness and well-being. He removed sin and sorrow from human hearts; he replaced despair with hope; to the hungry he fed the Bread of Life. Often too he had to nurse the wounded victims of the Bonaparte plague. He found food and shelter for them. And he taught them to realize their human destiny, not by crying: "*Vive L'Empereur!*" but by crying as they touched Christ with re-won faith, "My Lord and My God!"

To save souls was the Curé's absorbing "hobby." How much joy he won by his hobby and how remunerative it was! The Church takes note of it in the prayer of the Mass in his honor: "May we be enabled to gain for Christ the souls of our brethren and with them attain to everlasting glory."

Napoleon Bonaparte died in loneliness in St. Helena. He was forsaken, dethroned, and in part forgotten. He had failed beyond the hope of a comeback. His doctor, an Irishman from Cork, tried to be kind to him and cheer him, with a French that belonged to the river Lee. But few cared any more. Christ "puts down the mighty from their seats."

In Ars, when his time came to die, the old Curé

was surrounded by a loving flock that derived from all parts of France. He didn't want honor but he couldn't escape it. Christ "exalts the humble!"

We may not at all need to be reassured in regard to our faith, but, did we have such a need, the Curé of Ars is there for us to see. We do need, however, in regard to faith, thoughts to make it grow and examples to fan it into activity. And the Curé of Ars can help a lot in that respect. But perhaps his greatest help for our faith will be in increasing our love for faith, for certainly he loved it well, and clung to it.

CHAPTER XII

MY DEBT TO ST. AUGUSTINE

I AM indebted to saints of many nationalities. For example, I have good friends overseas — deathless friends, though all are long since buried. In Spain, I have Teresa of Avila; in Italy Anthony of Padua; in France John Vianney, of whom I have just spoken, and Thérèse of Lisieux and Nicholas Herman. There is a good Dutchman, Thomas Hemerken of Kempen to whom I owe much, and many and great are the favors bestowed upon me by two fellow Dubliners, Columba Marmion and Willie Doyle. Out of Africa I have but one friend, one helper to boast of, Augustine of Hippo — my indebtedness to him is too great to pass over in silence.

There are special reasons why St. Augustine is a friend of mine. From him I got the authority to teach that we can and do touch Christ, and touch Him *well* (*bene* is Augustine's word), by faith. Then he showed me how it was all right, and the way of Providence, to be led back to Christ from a wicked life, by quite casual, trivial little experiences, that is, by concealed miracles. Lastly, I felt deep sympathy with Augustine, because he had to face the trying, embarrassing problem of whether or not he ought to write about himself. Should he, or should he not, expose his soul and its secrets to the world? Does a man imperil his friendship with Christ by discussing it in public? I thank Augustine for finding the answer to this puzzling question.

So, first about those *Confessions.** Augustine was in great doubt whether or not he should satisfy the curiosity of his friends and contemporaries by telling them about himself. He notes: "What I now am, at the very time of making these confessions, divers desire to know, who have or have not known me."

How intelligible to us today is his remark: "This race is curious to know the lives of others; slothful to amend their own." We read all kinds of crime stories, eager to learn about the dirt, but with never a thought of profiting personally, and improving ourselves, through learning about sin and misfortune.

Augustine continues: "What have I to do with men that they should hear my confessions — as if they could heal all my infirmities? . . . Why seek they to hear from me, what I am, who will not hear from Thee (Oh God), what they themselves are? And how know they, when from myself they hear about myself, whether I speak truly?"

Augustine prayed hard for guidance as to whether or not to write his "true story," and for light to see what object would be gained by it. In the end he understood that it would serve others and benefit them to hear about his conversion.

---

* *Harvard Classics,* Vol. 7, "The Confessions of St. Augustine," trans. by Ed. F. Pusey, Collier & Son, 1909.

As is well known there was some trouble and a division in Augustine's family. His mother Monica (St. Monica) was devout, but seemingly to some extent "a devouring mother." "She loved my being with her," writes Augustine, "as mothers do, but much more than many." Evidently Augustine was very conscious of maternal pressure.

Monica, however holy, was not very successful in explaining the faith to her son. She couldn't have been very good at expounding doctrine, for we find Augustine confessing to ignorance of and wrong ideas about the faith in spite of Monica's lessons. He writes later: "The Catholic faith teaches not what we (Manichaeans) thought and vainly accused it of."

When he decided to leave Africa for Rome, Augustine had no little difficulty in escaping from his mother, although he was well of age at the time. When he did succeed she followed him: and later, when he left Rome for Milan, Monica was still at his heels. Unlike most "devouring mothers," Monica tried to force Augustine into a marriage at Milan, but he successfully resisted her. What she considered best for him was not best in the eyes of Providence. Had she had her way the Church would have been deprived of one of her greatest lights. Monica's holiness did not give her the power to see into the future; nor did her love for her son always help her judgment in his regard. But he loved her, and admired her, and heard from her dying lips the consoling admission that he had been dutiful to her.

To return now to some of the stages or events that led up, in an incoherent way, to Augustine's conversion. In Africa, as a Manichee, he was a "party member," and his "party" in its conduct and philosophy was not wholly unlike the Communist Party in America. Members held together and followed a "line." They were materialists in a sense, who however co-equated God and the devil as co-eternal. Augustine, as a Manichee could not conceive of a spiritual substance. He said: "I knew not how to conceive except corporeally." Everything, for him, had to be extended in space. "When I wished to think on my God," he wrote, "I knew not what to think of but a mass of bodies, for what was not such did not seem to me to be anything." Though he had a strange reverence for God he denied Christ's divinity as unseemly and impossible. "It seemed to me unseemly to believe Thee (God) to have the shape of human flesh, and to be bounded by the bodily lineaments of our members."

His brilliant, restless mind struggled in vain to find truth. "No truth can be comprehended by man," he cried, in apparent despair. What was sin, for Augustine, but a natural reaction? Evil was a gross mass, uncreated by God, but unbounded. He had not found the answers that his mind sought.

"What are the answers?" he demanded of other "party" members. They told him that Faustus was coming. Faustus, a brilliant Manichee, would have all the answers for Augustine. "Have patience, fellow, you'll soon have the 'party line' and it will satisfy you!"

Faustus came and lectured, a skillful, eloquent, and likable man with a certain honesty. But he failed to explain to Augustine the things he wanted to know. And, in some respects, he was ignorant. "Faustus was ignorant of those arts in which I thought he excelled," said Augustine, but, "he was not altogether treacherous to himself, for he was not altogether ignorant of his own ignorance."

The Faustus fiasco was a shock to Augustine and he began to have serious doubts about "the party." Then he fled to Rome, and from Rome he went to Milan, where he had to meet the great Bishop Ambrose. Augustine liked the Bishop. "That man of God received me as a father . . . thenceforth I began to love him . . . not as a teacher of truth but as a person kind toward myself."

Here once again the eternal truth confronts us: human kindness is the best first step on the road to the spiritual kindness of introducing a soul to Christ.

Augustine, a lover of eloquence, often heard Ambrose preach "for the how, not the what of his sermons." He would have liked to chat with Ambrose but Ambrose was too busy and he kept the young man waiting. In fact, Ambrose more or less ignored Augustine, as he did the devout Monica, who, I think, wearied him.

Augustine was not without good friends, honest serious-minded boys, who like him were searching for truth. He lived with two of them, Alypius and Nebridius. Sometimes there were visitors, and on occasion these happened to be Christians.

One day Augustus met a happy drunk on the street. It was a most extraordinary stage in his conversion! He watched the happy drunk and found himself envying his gaiety. "What he had obtained by means of a few begged pence," reflected Augustine, "the same was I plotting for by many a toilsome turning and winding: the joy of temporary felicity." Augustine was no drunkard himself, though he led a loose life. But he wanted to be carefree, to have peace of mind, and he thought the happy drunk was to be envied.

Augustine was, by this, impressionable. When a Christian friend, one Simplicianus from Rome, visited him, he heard from his visitor's lips the strange story of the conversion to Christianity of a great Roman called Victorinus. The story moved Augustine profoundly and he felt "on fire to imitate Victorinus."

About this time Augustine began to reflect on the injury that his self-indulgence was doing to his spirit. He began to understand that "the flesh lusteth against the spirit and the spirit against the flesh." He came to see the meaning of Paul's prayer: "Awake, thou that sleepest, and arise from the dead, and Christ shall give thee light" (Eph. 5:14). Augustine was now drifting, unconsciously, under the breath of the Holy Spirit. Anything might happen, any day! Grace was at work, and a small shock could give Augustine the sight his inner eye needed.

The small shock came when another Christian friend, Pontitianus, called on Augustine and Alypius. Like the

former visitor, Simplicianus, the new one had a strange
tale to tell. With two friends he had of late gone to
inspect a monastery where monks dwelt. While there he
had taken up a book on St. Anthony, the hermit, and
read it. His two friends did likewise, and they at once
determined to become monks.

Simplicianus must have told his story in a very dramatic
way for he had scarcely finished when Augustine jumped
up and cried: "What ails us, Alypius?" Then, hurrying
out into his garden, he threw himself on the ground
under a fig tree and began to pray as he had never
prayed before. And as he prayed he heard, or seemed
to hear, a young voice chanting: *"Tolle, lege! Tolle, lege!"*
— Take up (your book) and read!

Augustine had a copy of the New Testament in his
room. He rushed back to his room and opened the book
at random. There he read the one lesson of clean morality
that he needed: "Let us walk honestly as in the day, not
in rioting and in drunkenness, not in chambering and
impurities, not in contention and envy: But put ye on
the Lord, Jesus Christ, and make not provision for the
flesh in its concupiscences" (Rom. 13:13, 14).

Now Augustine understood why he had been unable
to see God. He had not been pure of heart. "Blessed
are the pure of heart for they shall see God."

Augustine and Alypius hesitated no longer. Monica's
mourning was "turned into joy." The voice that Augustine heard — was it one of those little miracles that can
never be proved, but that are so certain? And the famous

toothache that nearly killed him, and that mysteriously disappeared when he and his friends knelt to pray — was it too one of those little miracles? Of course, it was! Certain but unprovable!

No doubt Augustine's former friends, still belonging to "the party," laughed loud and long when they heard of his superstitious belief in voices and disappearing toothaches — and of his excitement over emotional conversions. But, whereas, Manichees were still unable to see and taste and feel God's goodness, Augustine was praying thus: "Not with doubting but with assured consciousness, do I love Thee, Lord! Thou hast stricken my heart with Thy word and I loved Thee. . . . Too late have I loved Thee, O Thou Beauty of ancient days, yet ever new! Too late I loved Thee. And behold Thou wert within and I abroad and there I searched for Thee. . . . Thou wert with me and I was not with Thee."

Soon Augustine was drawn toward Christ by that magnetism that every saint knows and feels. He wrote, "When I shall with my whole self cleave to Thee, I shall nowhere have sorrow or labor; and my life shall wholly live, as wholly full of Thee."

Chapter XIII

SCANDAL — AND THE GOLDEN RULE

CLEOPHAS was sad. He was discouraged and scandalized, as was his companion. He admitted as much to the Stranger that joined them, as they trudged away from Jerusalem to Emmaus. He had put his hope, his faith in "a prophet, mighty in work and word before God," but the prophet had let him down. "We hoped that it was he that should have redeemed Israel." Deceived and disillusioned, Cleophas saw that there was nothing to do but leave it all behind and flee. Then the Stranger intervened — explained — and love replaced scandal in Cleophas' heart! In the old and touching story of Emmaus (as told by Luke 24), we see Christ triumphant over scandal. Scandal causes woe, but it is not invincible. The love that Christ taught and exemplified can conquer scandal always no matter how heartbreaking it may be.

A prominent public figure, an exemplary Catholic, active in Church work, and, perhaps, a daily communicant, is investigated by a government office and is found to be a thief. A well-known Catholic athlete or a famous Catholic actress is revealed by the press to be at Reno in connection with divorce proceedings. A good and well-loved priest, "a prophet . . . in work and word . . .

93

before the people," abandons his parish and perhaps hits the press by taking up the Baptist ministry. Loyal Catholics, of the temper of Cleophas, grow sad at such news — that is inevitable. But if they allow themselves to be discouraged and scandalized, it is because of a lack of love, of Christlike love, in their hearts. Where Christ's love dwells, there is no fear. "Love drives out fear!" (Jn.)

To write about scandal is a difficult and humiliating task for me, but in a book like this, which deals with the subject of "stray shepherds" it has to be faced. The scandal of the traitor priest (or apostle) is as old as the Church itself: it goes back to the hour of the Last Supper. "One of you is about to betray Me."

The fact of Judas' betrayal was not hidden by the Evangelists; it could not be hidden. In this religious order or that; in this parish or that, when a priest deserts, the fact cannot be hidden. It becomes known; it is, of course, deplored; but it should not be the occasion of scandal to anyone who loves Christ and understands the economy of His redemption. He chose men, not angels, to carry on His work of salvation. When He decided to choose men, He foresaw that among those He chose there would be some who would fail Him.

He knew that there would be scandal, but He left us the means of overcoming scandal. He said: "Love one another!" Scandal was not to be undone by hate, by persecution, by the knife of a fanatic, or by the tongue of a bitter polemicist, but by love.

In the first place, love is a safeguard against impetuous, misplaced scandal. A saint goes into a tavern and plays a game of billiards with a roué — in public. Shocking? But no! You're going too fast. That "scandal giver" is Ignatius of Loyola and he's engaged in trying to win a soul for Christ.

Here is a snapshot of a young priest. He is sitting on a bench in a park, with his arm around a girl, and his head resting on her shoulder. I saw the picture myself. Shocking, was it not? I didn't think it shocking because I knew the priest, and I knew who the girl was. She was his sister: the best sister a priest ever had. In America he, an Irishman, had lost his grip and gone "on the road." But his sister in Ireland had kept after him with her letters and prayers, and had finally coaxed him home where he was able to clean up everything and get ready for a new start. She came with him to Cobh, to see him off on his steamer, and to make him renew as he parted from her, his earnest vow to be a new man, a new priest when he got back to the States.

A scandal, big or little, is always a trial of faith. It is as harsh a trial as is sudden sickness, or the stroke that an old person is subject to.

You go to confession and you find the confessor angry or suspicious. If you, foolishly, take scandal at the priest's human frailty (which may only be the result of a bad headache), you may, as many a silly person has done, give up going to confession. I remember a fine young businessman telling me that he had not gone to confes-

sion for years because a priest once had suspected him
of concealing a sin.

What but the love of Christ can smooth over difficulties and reject scandal? Sometimes in confession a priest
is sorely puzzled — as is well explained by the old story
of "Pat and the Cow."

"I stole a rope, Father!" Pat confessed.

"A rope?" the priest asked; then, suddenly suspicious,
he added, "Was there anything at the end of the rope?"

"There was indeed, Father!" Pat mumbled. "There was
an old cow!"

Love not only prevents us from prejudging others, but
it keeps us altogether from judging others. Even when,
with our eyes, we see what appears to be wrong, we
refrain from condemning a brother. It is God's preroga-
tive, not ours, to judge.

Not long ago I had a letter from a nun who had love
in her heart to sustain her grief. It was about a priest
that she wrote me; a priest who had suddenly disappeared
from the parish. "He was such a good, holy priest. I
don't know what can have happened. There was not a
breath of scandal against him. He just mailed his keys
to the Bishop and left. No one knows where he has
gone. Won't you pray? He was so very good."

That good nun sensed, no doubt, that a priestly failure
may have more behind it than appears; something that
is not to be accounted for by what an evil mind may
think. The human is a delicate creation; the nervous
system can take so much, and no more. In battle, in

strenuous activity, a shock may upset a man so as to undermine his self-control. Men flee under the effect of shell shock. They flee, not knowing why or where they are going.

I personally do not find it difficult to refrain from attributing an evil motive to a priest who suddenly quits. I have come in contact with strange manifestations of fear. I know what an overwhelming motive a sudden fear can be. I knew a priest once — he was at the time "on the road," as the expression goes — and he was (were it not for his timidity) one of the best priests one could meet. His story was hardly credible — but it was true. His Bishop, in the mid-West, had suddenly appointed him to an outlying parish. So he packed up and went to this place. When he arrived in the parochial house he was admitted by a buxom housekeeper who eyed him, as he thought, curiously. During the evening he found himself growing afraid of her, perhaps also suspicious of her. In the morning after Mass, he impulsively packed up and fled. He was too timid to face his Bishop to explain — so he kept on traveling until he arrived in Limerick City (Eire) where he got in touch with me. How foolish it is to condemn a man for cowardice when one is so totally unable to measure the fear that assailed him!

When one of our idols collapses — when one whom we had regarded as a saint betrays or seems to betray a cloven hoof — when we are frightened, scared to death, at the horrible reality of evil — that is the moment to

ask Christ: "Increase my faith, Lord! Increase my love!"
Instead of taking refuge in the "Oh! Oh!" of scandal —
instead of sharing in the delight of a whispering cam-
paign — stretch out your hand until it rests in Christ's
and say: "I believe! I love! I am not discouraged!"

The terrible thing about scandal is that it proliferates.
It grows by multiplication; it reproduces itself. Often
there was something that scandalized the very one who
comes to the forefront as a giver of scandal. There is in
scandal something in the nature of a vicious circle. In
one way or another, we all give scandal. Most of us
increase its evil effects by our tongues. Instead of obeying the law of love; instead of being charitable in our
judgments and remarks about others, we think ill and
speak ill. Instead of fighting against scandal we fight
to increase it.

I know that desertion from among the ranks of priests
is a cause of grievous scandal among the Catholic laity,
but they should not close their eyes to the fact that
good can survive even in a priest who runs away. I
believe entirely in a verse from the old Irish Book of
Lismore:

> O Christ! O Ruler of Battles!
> Woe to him that deserts his mighty Lord!

but it is my hope to lessen to some degree the scandal
that he, the deserter, gives.

It should not be imagined that many stray shepherds
use their pens or raise their voices against the Church.

As a matter of fact very few, a very insignificant percentage, do so. The common intention of stray shepherds is to avoid, as far as they can, the giving of scandal. Their impulse is to hide, to remain unknown, so that no one may be shocked by their presence or their new activities.

I knew one "ex" Order priest in New York City in the twenties, Father C., who was extremely poor. His only occupation, besides writing a few reviews which he signed with a pseudonym, was to hawk vacuum cleaners from door to door. At that time a man called Ford had a radio station in the city which he used to deliver belittling addresses against the Church. I spoke on Ford's radio a couple of times and he told me that he would be glad to pay any "ex-priest" (it was the word he used) who would be willing to speak for him. I told Father C. about Ford's offer. I remember the substance of his reply: "Look, Boyd! I'm poor. I'm practically penniless. But even if I were starving, I wouldn't talk against the Church!"

I have a good friend John, who in his youth belonged to an Order, and who, as he explains, through "philosophic doubts" about the faith, wandered so far as to accept a ministry in a Protestant church. In time his faith returned and he set himself to catholicize his congregation. He taught his flock to love and honor our Lady. Not a few of his people, under his influence, joined the Church — and members of his family became devout Catholics. Only some strange fear, some chronic hesitation, has delayed his own return. Not long ago, a lady (not aware that I knew John) wrote me about his leading her into the Church, and telling me that all her family were now Catholics. The particular cause of her writing to me was to find out how she could be of assistance to an old priest (whom she thought was mental) who seemed to be a homeless wanderer.

I could continue for pages, recording instances of actual apostolic zeal in priests no longer entitled to wear the collar; and not apostolic zeal alone, but outstanding charity. How God works good out of evil will always be a mystery to us!

CHAPTER XIV

GOOD OUT OF EVIL

I REFER continually to myself and to others in like state as "shepherds without sheep," but the term is not entirely accurate. As a matter of fact, we have sheep to care for; sheep that Providence herds in our direction. They are certain strays who are willing to come near us, and even to look to us for guidance.

It is a curious fact, but I think, incontestable, that some priests who quit their duty and hide away, while being unwilling to meet or consult with regular priests, that is with priests in good standing, are not unwilling to meet and consult with us shepherds without sheep. I know some of them, and others like me know them too. In this way we are given an opportunity of doing good; of turning to good account an unhappy evil.

From a letter, dated March 14, 1955, I take the following gem of Christian charity: "I regard anything I can do for stray shepherds as the most important thing I have to do in life." This statement, which would have become the lips of St. Pius X, or any other saintly bishop who had the salvation and sanctification of the clergy at heart, was actually written me by a brother shepherd without sheep. And it was not, on his part, the mere expression of a true desire. He has lived up to what he writes. A call to help a stray is a must call for him.

From my experience, there seems to be born in and with the repentance of a priest who has wavered and wandered, a sacred and touching impulse to aid fellow wanderers, and to help to bring them back to Christ. I would like to go even farther than this, and say from experience, that once a wandering priest begins to realize that he is on the road home, he begins to busy himself in a quiet way trying to get other wanderers to accompany him.

My book, *Shepherds in the Mist,* was the flowering in my mind and heart of the impulse, born on the occasion of my repentance, to help other wandering priests to reconsider how they were living, and what they were doing; and to take the road back to where they belonged. I have been told that several priests were moved by the appeal I made, and I sincerely hope it was so.

But it belongs to this chapter to record some detailed examples of how we wanderers strive to save others. There was, for instance, the noble effort an octogenarian Irish padre, J.H., made on my behalf. It merits to be retold.

J.H. lived in Canada, and it was from there that he began to correspond with me. At first he wrote as an ordinary layman, more or less approving my writings critical of the Church, but always tempering his approval with a 'but' or a 'perhaps.' He posed as a more or less independent type of Catholic, but, all the same, as solidly attached to the faith. Then, as our friendship grew, he showed his hand a little, and manifested solicitude about my spiritual well-being. Was I praying? Did I go to Mass? Did I ever think of looking around for an easy way of becoming reconciled? He took so much care to be tactful that I could not take offense at his practical interest in me.

He used to tell me about himself, how, in spite of Canada's winter, he never missed his cold shower in the mornings. He told me too how he used to pass hours in the waiting room of a railway terminal, talking, when occasion presented itself, to lonely bums and travelers. I think, now, that he was always on the lookout for *stray shepherds,* should Providence put them in his way.

A couple of years passed before he finally revealed in a long and moving letter how he, like myself at this moment, was a 'ghost priest,' who had, however, sought and obtained forgiveness from Rome. He told me how happy he was over his reconciliation — how easy it had proved to be — and how he was always praying that I would do as he had done. This letter was a great surprise to me, and a great grace. We remained good friends until his death. God rest his soul; this is my daily prayer.

There was another old priest, a scholarly, dignified man living in retirement whom I used to visit at his sister's request, so as to be of service if the problem which troubled him was amenable to psychological treatment. My contacts with him began on the eve of my leaving the Jesuit Order, and we soon became good friends. He was not communicative, but always he was very friendly and we played many a game of chess together. I could see that he nursed indignant resentment over some real or imagined wrong that had been done him. He was hurt deeply; his soul seemed to be chilled. Nonetheless he took an interest in me, and I feel sure he was concerned about my welfare. It must have come as a great shock to him to learn that his young priest-friend had followed him "into the mist." Perhaps in some way he blamed himself for this, and determined to make amends as well as he could.

Not long after leaving my Order I learned that this good old man had gone back to work as pastor in his parish. I think this was a dramatic instance of "good out of evil": of charity felt in one priestly heart for the heart of a fellow wanderer.

The most mysterious of my contacts, at the time that I was practicing as a psychoanalyst in New York City, was with a genial, kindly little man, T.G. He told me that he was retired from business, that he had prospered, and that he was living with his mother on Long Island. He was a man of amazing erudition. He seemed to have read everything and apparently remembered everything he ever read.

I saw a good deal of T.G. and came to appreciate his charm and generosity, no less than his learning. On his part he came to know my friends, many of whom were stray shepherds. In these he took a very great interest and he went out of his way to help them. For some he secured jobs; to others he gave financial assistance. He was always ready and willing to do anything for a stray shepherd. He had for them the kind of love that St. Peter Claver had for colored slaves.

As I came to know T.G. better I discovered that he was a man of faith and prayer, a devout practicing Catholic. Also I could not but notice that he exercised a beneficial, steadying influence on the more reckless of my friends.

Years went by and our friendship continued. Even when I came to live in California we remained united through frequent letters. And when the time came that I announced to him that I was reconciled to Holy Church, no one was more happy than he.

A few years more and T.G. fell ill. Then troubles of various kinds overwhelmed him, but his faith and joyous spirit never failed. The time came when it was a rare adventure for him to be able to creep from his room and struggle step by step for a visit to his parish church to call on Christ whom he loved.

When two years ago, his holy death came, I was deeply grieved and my prayers for him were fervent. He had been a good friend to a number of stray shepherds; we owed him much. In time, too, my prayers though fervent were to be redoubled, for a few months ago I discovered to my astonishment, and I confess to my immense joy, that in his early years, T.G. had stood, as I had stood at the altar of God, offering Holy Mass!

My friend had been, without my ever suspecting it, a shepherd without sheep, a ghost priest, and — how could I doubt it? — a saint!

It should not strain the imagination of readers of this book to picture a hermit-priest old, alone, embittered by the tragedy of his life, struggling to survive in his poverty, and resentful and suspicious of all interference. How many such there are in this country, who can tell? Once in a while I receive news of such a one.

There was J.M., in his seventies and growing blind. A Catholic layman, living in his neighborhood, managed to find out about him and offered help. But his offer was rejected. This layman then wrote to me. He said J.M. was often seen at Mass, and saying his rosary, seated at the door of his hovel, but that he was bitter and impossible to approach.

It happened that I was in touch with "one of my own" who lived not far distant and I told him about J.M. As I anticipated, he took up the case at once. He visited J.M. and was surprisingly well received. Soon they became quite friendly, and J.M. was persuaded to accept an electric heater for his hovel and a few other little gifts.

Then my friend broached the idea of an operation for J.M.'s eyes, and guaranteed that there would be no fee. At first J.M. agreed, but later, when he learned that he would have to leave his shack and stop in a hospital, he grew suspicious and refused. All he had to live on was the old age pension and he was afraid that if he moved away from where he was living his little pension would be stopped. When a man is old and suspicious no human persuasion avails; at times it is best to leave an old man with his rosary beads to face the future in his simple, if clouded, faith.

The shepherd without sheep, the unfrocked, laicized priest avoids publicity. Instinctively he keeps out of sight as far as he can. His place is not at Catholic social gatherings, nor at Church meetings. He has to be wary about exciting notice, and provoking the question: "Who is he?" Often he can do good by correspondence, or by writing little articles (if he is able to do so). A correspondent or an author remains, largely, a faraway unknown — a recluse, so to say. But in spite of his effort to lie low, his pastor, at least, will know about the ghost-priest and it may happen that a wise pastor will, on occasion, be able to use him for good. It is in order that pastors may consider the possibility of handing over to a shepherd without sheep, whom they trust, the bit of work that he is qualified to do, that I record the incident that follows.

One afternoon my pastor phoned to ask me if I could call upon him as he had a visitor whom he wanted me to meet. I drove down at once to my pastor's house and he brought me into his study and introduced me to a fellow countryman, a man in his late thirties, dressed in lay clothes. I guessed, instinctively: "A priest in trouble — a stray shepherd!" and, of course, I was right.

We chatted a while, and then my pastor suggested

that his visitor and I should go for a drive and a chat. As we were leaving, he took me aside for a moment, as he felt for his pocketbook. But I shook my head. Then the stray and I left.

We had a long chat. It was easy for my new friend to tell me all for he knew I would understand. He spent the night, at my suggestion, in a motel near where I live. Early next morning I picked him up, and that evening, thanks to the generosity of the pastor of a nearby city, he had his ticket and was on his way to a temporary home.

In one way or another a ghost priest can be useful, can even face a chore that a regular priest, dressed in clericals, could not face.

One day the superior of a little convent phoned to ask me if I could come to see her, as she had a very difficult problem and perhaps I could help. It happened that she had been asked to visit a very sick and very rebellious Catholic to try to do something for him before he died. In her charity, accompanied by another sister, she visited this man and found him full of ill-will against the Church and badly prepared.

While she tried to quiet him down, she noticed on a table beside his bed a notorious book, purporting to be written by an "ex-priest." Anxious to get this book away from the sick man she asked him if she might take it. Then she slipped it into her bag. Some time later she received a message from the man demanding back his book at once. It was then that she got the idea that he was a stray shepherd who had turned sour on the Church.

Sister told me the story, handed me the book, and revealed her suspicion that the man was a priest who had gone astray. I promised to call to see him and to do what I could: I assured her that I'd soon find out whether or not he was a true priest.

I called on the man next day, and my visit was far from pleasant. He pretended that he was an "ex-priest" but when I challenged him to repeat even a few words of the sacramental *formulae* that no priest could ever forget he was completely unmasked. He was no more than a preacher who had been employed by some anti-Catholic organization to "reveal" the hidden horrors of Rome. I gave him back his book; I had to do so. I pointed out some of the lies it contained, but the result was that he raised his voice, whereupon another unpleasant character came into his room. Angry voices invited me to leave and I did so. I was glad, meanwhile, that no regular priest had been subjected to the indignity of the adventure.

That good comes out of evil when God so wills it was brought home to me, not long ago, by the remark of a Protestant friend. This friend is one whom I respect very much, a man of great honesty and charity. It is rarely that we touch upon religion when we chat, but of late we did so, and a remark he made both surprised and interested me. He said: "One thing I find about Catholics has impressed me very much. It is the fact that Catholics, and I have known a few such, who give up the Catholic Church — and join another religion — will still return again and live as devout Catholics!"

Once a priest always a priest — is repeated over and over again, everywhere in the world. Not only is it a true saying in regard to its surface meaning but it contains also a deep truth that is hidden.

A priest may become a renegade — a scandal — but be patient! Give him time! Rather, give the grace of God time to do its work. Renegade priest though he seem to be, the day comes when he will act out the character of a good priest — he will absolve some dying sinner though he be a tenant of Hell's Kitchen — or he will baptize the suffocating babe of some poor woman of the streets. As God is God, there will always be the blossoming of good from evil.

Chapter XV

CAN A SHEEP SAVE A SHEPHERD?

IN THE chapter, just finished, I have discussed the ways in which one priest, albeit a hidden shepherd, helps or tries to help shepherds in still greater distress than he. And, no doubt, the thought has occurred to some readers: "Is the work of helping stray shepherds the exclusive privilege of other shepherds? Is there no role for the layman or laywoman, the mere sheep, in this work of love and mercy?" I will attempt now to answer that question.

A distinguished Jesuit, Father John LaFarge, in writing an appreciation for the jacket of my book, *Shepherds in the Mist,* outlined the role of the sheep in the sanctification and in the saving (when "lost") of the shepherd. He wrote:

> To every priest comes often the humbling thought that he owes his perseverance not to his own merits, but to the prayers of devoted souls who intercede and make sacrifices on his behalf. With this thought comes the natural longing that these same graces may be extended to all who have strayed from the path of their vocation and the wondering query as to what he or his brother priests or all the faithful can do to bring them back.

In Holy Scripture we have the touching picture of the shepherd seeking and saving the sheep that was lost. We have, too, the no less moving picture of the sheep (the Good Samaritan) saving another sheep. But, is there in Scripture any hint of approval of a sheep trying to "rescue" a shepherd?

I find, though it may be only a pious fancy, such a hint in the scene where Magdalen, the sheep, is seeking for the Prince of Shepherds, at the empty tomb. He is "lost"! How can she find Him and rescue Him? "Sir!" she says to a presumed kidnaper, "if thou hast taken Him hence, tell me where thou hast laid Him, and I will take Him away" (Jn. 20:15). Was the humble and loving Magdalen destined by God to teach other sheep to seek and to rescue lost shepherds of the days to come?

When Christ established His Church, He chose men, frail humans, as the shepherds of His flock. In their hands He placed the future of His kingdom on earth. In so doing He did not risk its fate. He knew that all would be well; that the gates of hell would not prevail. But He foresaw that some, perhaps many, of His shepherds would prove faithless.

But though some, or many, should fail Him, Christ did not ordain that such weaklings should be abandoned to their fate. For them, as for all sinners, His heart was full of compassion. There was to be mercy, forgiveness, and even a blessed "home-coming" for them too. And this promise He made through the lips of Luke, when the evangelist wrote in describing the scene at Bethlehem:

"And the shepherds returned, glorifying and praising God."

We call them "stray shepherds," those priests whom we know of who have fled from their duties and no longer labor in Christ's vineyard. They are still and always will be priests; they are still ours. Their claim on our love, on our charity, is great. They are the brothers, sons, friends of our very own; our own brothers and friends, it may be. We pray for them; we yearn to help them; but to help is not, as we shall see, an easy task. To touch, to contact a rebel priest, is to touch a wounded man. What delicacy, what skill, what love is needed! "To a festering wound one must needs apply a gentle hand!" (Pindar.)

The task of contacting and trying to help a stray shepherd is not to be lightly undertaken. Always there is the danger of hurting, rather than healing the soul of the one we most sincerely wish to help. To interfere in his life with make-believe interest and cordiality — with synthetic love — is worse than useless. He detects with ease what is not true love. But, on the other hand, God may, most unexpectedly, put it in your way to be of service to some stray shepherd. An old friendship may be renewed; a new sincere friendship may be begun; and you find yourself linked with one who is not, but should be, closely linked with Christ.

The feeling, the mind, the outlook of the stray shepherd is largely misunderstood. There are common false prejudices in his regard. Some whose Catholicism is tinged with Jansenism — and I regret to have to say that some of my Irish fellow countrymen belong to this class — harbor bitterness and antagonism against him. They speak of him even as "the priest nobody wants." They think, always, of him as a potential foe of the Church. But, surely, it is incumbent upon us, before we attempt to help him, to try to understand him and to eschew all false prejudices and suppositions.

To begin with, we must rid ourselves of the unfair and baseless idea that in shedding his clerical garb he deliberately divested himself of all his goodness. The likelihood, amounting almost to certainty, is that, whatever his "grouse" may be, he still cherishes the faith, prays with fervor to God and to our Lady, tries to be honest and kind. I have personally known enough strays, both during and after my two decades "in the mist," that I feel qualified to reject, as absurd, the notion that they are wont to shed their virtues and good qualities overnight.

And what of the notion that a stray is a potential enemy of the Church? Is he willing and ready to attack the Church in exchange for a little publicity and a small dole?

It is true that a few, relatively a very few, when forced by sheer want and the cruel pressure of circumstances, indulge in abusing and libeling the Church. But the vast majority — and I know it so well — whatever their faults may be, forswear any attack on their religion and avoid the giving of scandal with all their power.

That is their point of honor. As one poor stray, from my own city of Dublin, whispered to me with tears in his eyes: "In spite of everything I've suffered, I never did or said a single thing against the Church!"

Do those who think harshly of stray shepherds ever pause to make allowance for the vagaries of the human mind? Do they face honestly their own wretched habits of self-excuse and of self-justification? We shirk our duties and we plead ill health. We overcharge in business and plead "a rising market." We resent a slight with fury and hate on the ground of maintaining our dignity.

Like us, the stray shepherd seeks, and with the assistance of sophistry — just as we do — finds some seeming ground for self-justification. He tells himself that the injustice he suffered was "too great to bear." He ascribes his uncanonical "escape" to a fear and a loneliness that he could not face. Or he may have recourse to the specious excuse, with which, in my time, I tried to deaden my conscience: "If I had stayed on, I would have gone mad!"

In adjudging the wrongdoing of the stray, we should always bear in mind that, though he betrayed a "faithful God's great love," he was, in part, devil-tricked into doing so. He, as is every priest, was the target of direst temptation. He was wounded; he succumbed; but is it for us to judge?

To understand a stray shepherd we should not think of him as being in utter bad faith, but rather as very sensitive, hurt, and desirous of being left alone. He tends to hide from those he has known; to live among strangers. He wants "his secret" to be kept. He feels he has a right to his secret, and when a fellow Catholic betrays to those among whom he now lives that "So-and-So *was* a priest," he is terribly hurt and embarrassed. Many a stray has had to quit his job, where he was doing good, honest work, because some thoughtless Catholic "told."

And now, if I could only tell it with emphasis and appeal, I would reveal the important fact of the chain that binds the stray to the good and happy past. That chain is there, emotional in part, nostalgic too, but factual. The past is a part of his inner self, and he does not want to lose it. He hasn't forgotten home, friends, old times. In his loneliness and exile they mean a lot to him. He hopes against hope that he is still remembered; still loved; and that there are those back home who, somehow, "don't blame him."

Any Catholic who wants to help a stray should aim to strengthen that chain: to keep old memories pleasantly and tactfully alive; to make the stray feel, as far as he can, that he is as much loved as he ever was.

To take a case: suppose that John, who knew Father Tom well in the old times, meets him on the street dressed in lay clothes. John knows his story. They stop for a chat. How is John to act? Is he to put on a sour face and say: "It's sad for me, Father, to meet you like this"? Is he, with great piety, to tell Tom how he prays for him every day? What good, on earth, will a "holier than thou" attitude on the part of John do?

It seems to me that John should act with kindness and sense. He should tell Tom how glad he is to find him; he should tell him bits of news about mutual friends; he should act as though Tom were still his same old self and nothing changed. He should suggest, if there be the means of so doing, that they meet again for lunch or to go to a ball game.

If after their chat Tom is inclined to say to himself: "John is all right; he is still a good friend; thank God he doesn't look down his nose at me but likes me as well as ever," John has done his part well.

The danger inherent in hurting the feelings of such a one is that he is prone to turn his bitterness into hate. If you insult a stray shepherd, you do the devil's work, even when you mean well by your hard words! He is, so to say, "on the defensive," and it is an approach that is peaceful, not a provocative one, that is best. In my days "in the mist" I had a few unhappy experiences of tactless "zeal."

There was a young priest who wrote to me to denounce my conduct in harsh, uncouth words. His letter concluded by telling me how he yearned to give me a good kicking.

The letter did me no good. It only increased my bitterness. He may have felt good and "inspired" to write the letter. His subsequent career seemed to show that he was an excellent priest. But, why? Why? Has not St. Peter warned us plainly to "respect all men"?

Another priest who visited me on business told someone, who in turn relayed to me what he said, that while with me he felt he was in the presence of the devil! It is not the devil that one should see in a stray but the face of the wounded, bleeding Christ!

I have said enough of wrong ways of approaching a stray shepherd. Of right ways, many are, though right, insufficient. A casual attempt "to sweep the sinner off his feet" by one pretty effort is no use.

One young Jesuit, who said that he attributed his vocation to me, sent me, on hearing of my defection, a little Madonna picture that I had once given him. He added a few words; they were kind and well meant: "Remember old times!" It was a nice gesture, but *was there much love and sacrifice back of it?*

Another, a wise and clever priest, started to write me interesting newsy letters — he had the right idea: to keep me tied up with the past — not to censure me or prod me but, on the contrary, to assure me by indirection of his trust and confidence. This friend continued his splendid effort on my behalf for several months and I was deeply affected. But, alas! he lacked the patience and the self-sacrifice, the long enduring charity, that is called for in overcoming resistance to grace in the heart of such a one. He suddenly stopped writing to me. Another link with my happy past was gone!

Curiously, it is the admonition of John the Baptist that a sheep anxious to help a lost shepherd should keep ever in mind: "Prepare you the way of the Lord!" The sheep's victory lies in "reducing the resistance" of the shepherd and in opening the way for grace to act. By kindness and tact, enduring over the years, the sheep achieves this goal. Patience is "full of victory"; by patience I mean the slow way of love!

How telling on the heart of a stray shepherd is the sublime art of a good, understanding mother! While she does not condone the rebellion of her priest son, she does not accuse — and she does not "nag." The trust and the respect, mingled with the love that she shows toward him, are true. She does not indulge in self-pity, bewailing her brokenheartedness. It is to cheer her son, to keep alive his faith and courage, that she aims. For fourteen years, until her holy death, the attitude of my mother toward me was bright and trustful — with never a word of blame. In my poor mind I put her above St. Monica.

Perhaps the most instructive picture I can give, as to how a layman can help a stray, lies in the story of one good friend I had in my darkest days. This friend was A.N. He is now dead; God rest his soul. A.N. was a good and pious Catholic, a daily communicant. He was a man of great culture and charm; his easy success as a salesman resulted in his having time on his hands, no little share of which he spent on me.

As we became friends, he made it clear that he liked and valued my friendship. Often we lunched together; often he dropped into my office for a smoke and a chat. Always he proved entertaining, and never on any occasion did he criticize me or my ways. Though the books I wrote and the lectures I gave at the time must have shocked him very much, he cheerfully took everything for granted. He treated me as though I were *sans reproche,* the while he preached to me in one way only: by his splendid example of honor, faith, and charity. This friendship, which prepared the way of the Lord in my heart, lasted for four or five years and would have continued longer but that God called A.N. to his reward.

Is it too fanciful to put on the lips of A.N. (as he knelt in prayer in those days and thought of me) the words of Magdalen at the tomb: "Tell me where thou hast laid him and I will take him away"?

There are stray shepherds who have, in their confusion of mind and near despair, joined other churches; there are strays who have become addicts to drugs and alcohol and gambling; there are strays who have contracted marriage, by law of the land, and who have families to support; but there is none among them all who cannot be helped back to the welcoming arms of Christ.

The wound in the mystic body, the wound that was opened the night of the Last Supper by the first shepherd who betrayed, is a wound that calls for the loving care of Christ's sheep as well as of His faithful shepherds.

Chapter XVI

A DOG, A ROSE, AND
A GLASS OF OLD WINE

Praying for ever to the King
Who makes the sun shine . . .
Raiment and food enough for me,
From the King of fair fame,
And I to be sitting for a while,
Praying God in every place.
                    (Irish, tenth century.)

GOD knows the duality of our nature, and He provides.
He is "the Father of the poor" and "the Giver of gifts."
Dwell thoughtfully on any one of His gifts: a dog, a
rose, a glass of old wine, and you will realize, with St.
Bernard, that Christ has not only a look that wins you
(*dulcis in facie*) and a charm in His voice (*dulcis in
ore*), but the things He makes (and gives you) are ex-
ceedingly sweet (*dulcis in opere*).

Men talk to us by words and signs and what they say
is often obscure, and, still oftener, not worth hearing.
God talks to us by His gifts and what He says is clear
and satisfying. He tells us plainly, "The works that I do
in the name of My Father, they give testimony of Me"
— of the Goodness and Love that I am.

A little while ago Bran's companion, my Kerry Blue,

121

Nie, died. She was stubborn and often cranky, but never was she unfaithful. Brown-eyed, and brave, willful and playful, she did her bit of work well. She watched and barked and drove off cats and stray dogs that did not belong to the place. She stuck to her principles; she didn't change. "Small things," said Pascal, "are not small if great things come from them." A little dog can do a great lot for a man.

She is lying now, up there in her simple grave under an oak tree, with an upright pine staff at her head, and bright red bricks around her — but in my memory her lively dark face and short cocked ears are alert to welcome her master with demonstrations of delight and a furiously wagging tail. Always she thrilled to see him; always she was content to be with him; not because he was rich or handsome, but because he belonged to her. That was Nie.

Did she want any other home? Did she crave for freedom to tour the world on her own? To lead her own life? If so, she never betrayed such desire. Three times a day, or oftener, in weather that was sometimes wet and cold, for the ten quick years of her life, I brought her out for a run in the fields. Eleven thousand times we passed together through the old wooden gate. Not less often — indeed much oftener — there were tasty snacks for her to eat. When lights went out at night a big, cozy chair awaited her; when, as would happen in the fall, "foxtails" worked their way into her paws, there was a competent Vet to relieve her pain.

It was good to have her around, and she well repaid any little trouble taken on her behalf. Of course, there were times I had to coax her to come on out when the ground was muddy and the rain falling, for she hated to get wet. Early rising, too, as she grew older, had less appeal for her.

What does a dog mean to a man? What need in man for a dog did God foresee when he gave man this wondrous, lovely gift?

Well, there's companionship in a dog, a devoted and indeed unselfish companionship. I don't think that Darwin's inexorable law of evolution explains the role a dog is fitted to play in a man's life. I see mind, design (that is, divine design) in a dog's capacity to serve man.

A dog not only accompanies but he protects. He protects from tangible danger; he protects from intangible fears.

A dog, and this is perhaps his highest role, prompts man to be kind and considerate, to exercise his power of love. A happy dog is a lesson in the worth-whileness of sacrifice.

When I looked down at little Nie (and also, of course, when my eyes rested on Bran), I felt an implicit invitation to be good and kind. God speaks to me through the eyes of a dog, calling on the good impulses of my heart. It's not hard for me to see a glimmering of God's glory and majesty in His living creatures. After all, do we not read in the *Te Deum:* "The earth is full of the majesty of God's glory"?

When Nie grew gradually more and more sick, the fear that no human skill could save her oppressed me. I turned to St. Francis of Assisi and begged him to save her. I knew he would understand. While he did not grant my main request, he was not indifferent to it. Nie died without any pain or distress; she died gallantly like the little lady she was. And at her death, to make it easier to bear it, there befell me (no doubt, from St. Francis' hands), a marvelous spiritual favor, a despaired-of hope fulfilled.

One who aims at living close to Christ, at following Him faithfully, devotedly, and at wishing for nothing else, has a prototype in a good dog. Might one not wish to be Christ's dog, always happy to be at His heels, eating out of His hand, protecting Him as far as may be, seeking no other friend but Him?

> I'd gladly be an aging hound,
> Unleashed, but by devotion bound,
> To Christ, my kind, good Master.
>
> And every time He'd call to me
> Upwards I'd spring, and joyfully,
> I'd race, faster and faster.
>
> I'd lie content in any place,
> If I could only glimpse His face
> And ne'er would fear disaster.
>
> (Old Verses.)

On this hilltop roses grow well and abundantly. They are so very fair that it is difficult to choose the fairest

among them. Reds, yellows (golden yellows), whites
and in-betweens. I have a white that is utterly white;
not a cold dead white like the gift of the winter sky,
but warm and living. Every day that I look at roses and
rest my eyes in their loveliness I find more inspiring
color and form and harmony than I can take in.

For me they seem to move, to play, to smile in childlike innocence. They are guileless and generous, giving
gladly all they have. They have no secrets, nothing to
conceal; they trust in you to replenish their trivial needs.

I suppose one grows to understand roses better, or to
hear more clearly God's voice speaking through them.
Always He is present in His gifts. For me the day came
when, as it were, I found a rose for the first time; I was
able to touch its beauty; it moved before my inner eye;
it said the only word it knew: God!

How the beauty of a rose mocks science and man's
poor effort to conquer nature! How it puts man's pride
in its place! Who can measure, or weigh, or analyze the
charm there is in it? Frail and gentle rose, sweet in color,
graceful in form, what a gallant little witness you are
to the eternal Creator!

Over the radio comes harsh, threatening news, telling
of wrongs done and of wrongs contemplated; disturbing,
fear-provoking news. Outside in the shade of trees that
protect it against ruthless sunshine, the rose lives its
quiet dedicated life, protesting in its little way against
human crime. It is a promise of days to come when
"tears shall be no more."

Words, words — we pour out words about a rose while it would be more becoming to remain silent, absorbed in its reality, and in the reality of the divine glory it reveals.

For me, the rose grows forever in beauty as does Mary, the Mystical Rose, whom it symbolizes. It smiles in happiness. It shakes its pretty head, laughing, as a ripple of wind passes. It does not grieve that its day is short, for it lives out each one of its few hours perfectly. There's not a star but outlives the rose in length of days; but is there any star that gives any more glory to God than one, modest, gentle rose?

Here in California there is wine aplenty of every color and type. It is offered for sale in attractive bottles, with intriguing labels, at prices to suit every pocket. I have tried one kind and another, but always I am disappointed. It's old wine that I'm looking for; old wine that has not been doctored and debased by human hands. Old wine that is true wine, and pure; that renews and refreshes and has no exciting poison in it.

You need to be very honest with yourself, if you would make good wine. This I've tried to do. The grapes must be good and ripe; the barrels fresh and clean; the fermentation full and unhurried; you must add nothing whatever to sweeten or hasten or dilute or strengthen; at the right time you must change the wine from the barrel it was in to a fresh barrel, leaving the sediment behind. Then you must wait the full time of aging, for until then the wine is new.

Only old wine has, so to say, God's blessing on it; only it is worth while. This Christ Himself told us, saying: "And no man drinking old, hath presently a mind to new, for he saith: the old is better."

Often I dreamed of having a little cellar full of old wine, here on my hill, for the comfort that this wonderful gift of God affords — and for the hospitality it assures should a neighbor or a stranger drop in. But that dream has remained just a dream, and the "old wine" that I now yearn for is not the kind that wets the lips and helps one's words to run smooth. I know full well that the rich full juice of the vine, seasoned and prepared for man's use, belongs like a good dog or a fair rose among God's loving gifts that help us to know and love our Giver of Gifts; but I know, too, that when Christ said: "the old is better," His words had a mystical meaning for human hearts.

There was a wine I drank in my earliest days, when in utter trust and innocence I loved Christ, that I can no longer find. That "old wine" I drank so freely and so easily then, threw a roseate hue about all that happened, made music of voices, and gave even darkness a heartening glow. As I drank of Christ's love and goodness, I walked on the waves of a sunlit sea. Well, as say the Celts: "God be with the old days!"

But may I never again drink wine with Christ? Never again enjoy the divine stimulant He offers? The Psalmist assures me that all may again be well. "Return my soul where thy peace lies: the Lord hath dealt kindly with thee: He has saved my life from peril; banished my tears; kept my feet from falling. I will be the Lord's servant henceforward in the land of the living" (Ps. 114).

As my Lord's servant (returned), I will drink again; drink with more leisure, for life's hurry is over; and drink of the best, the very best, "the old wine." Christ wants me to drink of His love, and drink copiously. All the day He is tempting me to drink of this best wine: "Fill your glass!" He says, "Fill to the brim!"

I hear the song of a bird, a sudden song, and one new to my ears. That is Christ — saying: "Come, drink!"

A bright meteor, slow and soft, a round glow, crosses the sky before me at night. It fades away, but in its place there is the sound of Christ's voice: "Come and drink! Drink with Me!"

Here is a letter arriving. It is from a nun whom I have never seen, telling me, humbly and sweetly, of hours of prayer for me and for those I try to help. What is the letter but Jesus calling again? "Why don't you drink more of My love? Drink, My brother, drink!"

What if I obey the Psalmist (Ps. 104)? What will happen if I follow his advice? He says: "To the Lord betake you, and in Him find strength: evermore seek His face!" How else will my Jesus strengthen me than by giving me "a glass of old wine"? So may I live:

> Praying for ever to the King
> Who makes the sun shine. . .

Chapter XVII

MY PRAYER AND MY DREAM

MANY a time, while writing this book, I have looked up to Mary to ask her help. I did not, of course, see her — I have to wait a little while for that — but it may be a coincidence that the writing of this chapter happens on the feast day of one who saw her, face to face, and spoke to her. On this day, about a hundred years ago, little Bernadette Soubirous met Mary in the hollow of the rock of Massabielle. "She was," said Bernadette, "the loveliest lady I ever saw." Had we been there we should have said the same thing about Mary, and, no doubt, we should have asked: "Mother dear, what do you want?"

Why is Mary so near us? What does she want from us?

For my part, priest that I am, albeit in bonds, I know what she wants from me . . . and I find it hard to refuse her. From me, a priest, she wants faith: the strongest possible faith in her Son and in her. She wants the reign of Christ in my heart. As Abbot Marmion explained: "The reign of Christ — holiness through Him — is established in us in the measure of the purity, intensity, and fullness of our faith in Jesus Christ." It is not from me alone that Mary wants faith, but she wants it from all priests whether they walk in the light or stumble in the mist — and that is why, in this book, I tell all I know about faith.

It is faith that Mary wants from a priest more than anything else, for she sees that a priest's fidelity is dependent upon the firmness and sincerity of his faith. She knows that faith is the only antidote and preventive against treason in a priest. She has so often seen priests abandon Christ when their faith begins to grow cold. That "loveliest lady" who came to visit us, in the person of Bernadette of Lourdes, is in a special way the mother of priests, and she is deeply concerned about them, for she knows that the cause of Christ and the work of Christ lie in their hands. She knows that all depends upon their loyalty, which is, in effect, their faith. The prayer that she welcomes most of all from a priest's lips is this: "Lady, increase my faith!"

But what of priests who no longer say that prayer? There are priests today, many of them — and this is the saddest word written in this book — who are turning over in their troubled unhappy minds the pros and cons of casting aside their stoles and missals and deserting Christ. Fear, weariness, and the lure of the world is overwhelming their faith. They no longer open their eyes to see Christ; they are ashamed to look up into their Mother's face. If only, before they took the last grim, fateful step, they would come to her asking: "Lady, increase my faith!" and hear her answer, "My Son, I want you!"

When a good mother says: "My son, I want you!" what son can refuse to come?

I remember when a midnight telegram told me that my mother was dying and that she wanted to see me. I was an outcast priest, and there was little goodness in my heart, but the thought of my mother overrode all else. I was in the far North of Ireland and it was a long, rough way to Dublin, with a closed frontier to cross. But the journey was possible: that was all I cared about.

Through narrow, winding country lanes I drove hour after hour as fast as my car could go. I raced through towns and villages, up hills and down rocky valleys. There was never a light; only the savage barking of dogs.

"My mother, my mother!" I thought. Then there came to my lips the prayer that no priest, however lost he may be, forgets: "Mary, help me!"

It was already three hours past midnight when I found myself twenty miles from Dublin. There I ran into so thick and white a foggy mist that the reflected light from its whiteness made me think my car had caught fire. I got out of my car. There was no fire, but all around was dense moist white. Through this hopeless mist I drove on. I was doing only what any son would do.

An hour later the narrow road was blocked with cattle being herded into the market. Drovers cursed and shouted as I pushed the car through the milling calves. Then the light came and the road was wide, and soon after

I was at my mother's bedside — and in time. I knew she was pleased and happy as I gazed into her tired, tender eyes.

She was real — not a vision — a good mother who had sent me word: "I want you!" I was an outcast priest, still she had said: "I want you!" Mary is real too — not a vision — a good mother who sends word to every outcast priest — "I want you!"

"Lady, increase my faith!"

While I lived "in the mist" during two long decades, I met many brother strays. Every day I met them. With them I suffered the hardships and loneliness that belonged to our state. Together we learned the hopelessness of the struggle to be happy while carrying in our breasts, hearts that were never still. Together we grew more sensitive, more suspicious of well-wishers, more proud. Better than others we learned what it means to have no true home.

Those that I knew when I was among them, and those that I have since contacted, have somehow taken possession of my mind and my thoughts. They are forever with me as brothers and as friends. I think of them and pray for them; the prayer of my prayers is theirs, the prayer that is my very life. Morning, noon, and night, and fifty times between, I beseech Christ and Mary for them. I hope my dying lips will still be saying my ceaseless prayer: "Master, in Mary's name, look upon those priests who are about to die, and on all stray shepherds."

In the last few years while I was praying for those

priests (those strays) who are about to die, four of them died sudden deaths. One, whom I had invited to come to visit me, and who was deeply grateful for the invitation, was found dead in the room of a poor hotel, shot by his own hand. Another I knew well had the happiness of the sacraments at death.

Every morning, to keep my memory fresh, I tell Christ a long, long list of names: Gerry, Charlie, Bert, Bob, Peter, Tom, John, Joe, Fred, Francis, Don, Bill, Pat — and on and on. About each of them I could tell a moving story that would earn a fervent prayer. Many of them have taken first steps in their home-coming. God grant they finish at the altar!

Do some of them owe me money? Let them, if so, forget. Have some of them broken promises made me? Let them think that I have broken more promises than they ever did. Have I harsh thoughts in respect to any of them? Were I to nourish hard thoughts about anyone it would be about the coldhearted Catholic who speaks of them as "the priests nobody wants."

Maybe I could feel a bit unkindly about pious souls, if there be such, who remember to pray *only* for edifying, active priests. I would like to tell them about the Little Flower of Lisieux, who offered her last Holy Communion on earth, with fervor and tenderness, on behalf of a stray shepherd whom she knew!

The dream I have is to give all that is in me to the cause that Mary has certainly at heart; the cause that means help for stoleless, discredited priests, for priests in trouble.

First, there are casual little ways of giving help, if it only be by telling where real help can be obtained. Take, for instance, that priest about whose unconquerable faith I wrote, that "giant of a man" who came to see me in a terrible storm. I was able to give him news of a great and good Canonist, a Dominican Father, and soon after, he wrote to tell me, in thanks, how "it must have been his guardian angel that guided his steps to me, and through me to Father Z."

Sometimes my phone rings and an interview is arranged. One time it was Father B, with whom I had been dealing for a long time, and who had happily come to make his peace with Rome, though only as a shepherd without sheep. B is tall, handsome, and young, though his hair is gray. He dresses well, drives a fine car, and has a charm and persuasiveness of manner that has made him a successful salesman. But his heart is no longer in worldly success; he wants above all else to be "back in harness" as a priest.

B had a story for me of strange content. He said that when he had been superior of his religious house, one of his subjects, a Father John, got into trouble and, in spite of all B could do, went into the mist. For five years John was not heard of; then he came back, repentant, and was in time given a parish where he is doing great good. Meanwhile, B himself began to waver and, losing his self-control, left his Order.

"Well, Boyd," said B, as we sat sipping our coffee in a quiet place, "I felt so happy of late, being permitted once again to frequent the sacraments and serve Mass, that I thought I ought to write John to tell him the good news about myself. I knew he'd be glad. So I wrote him, and what do you think. Two days later he phoned me, long distance. He told me that my letter had made him weep for joy, and he said he was selling his car so as to be able to send me a little help which I might need. What a job I had to explain to him that I was O.K. financially!"

Again and again, I have come across instances, like that of John, where one priest, who has known trouble, is ready to do anything at all in his power to help out another who has also suffered.

There is Don, for example, who lives in this state and holds a very important position. He corresponds with me and has promised me to let me know the instant Rome decides on his case. Once, in a manuscript that I sent him to read, he noticed a reference to an old, sick, Irish priest — a somewhat embittered veteran — who was living in wretched circumstances in a shack on waste lands near a city. Don wrote me at once to inquire how he could help this brother of ours. "I'll get him medical care and supply all he needs," wrote Don, "and if I had an extra room in my house I'd try to persuade him to come and live with me."

In wishing to offer a home to a stray shepherd, Don touched upon the wish that should be in the heart of every true Catholic. He touched upon what is the ideal form of help that is needed, as a means of winning back Christ's lost shepherds. To put it as simply as I can, when stray shepherds, moved by grace, want to come back, they need to have some place where they will be welcome — where they will be received with open arms — where they can rest and pray.

There is, as all should know, one such home, a splendid one in every respect. It is called *Via Coeli*, and is situated at Jemez Springs, New Mexico. It is under the spiritual and material care of the Servants of the Holy Paraclete, a clerical congregation of diocesan right, authorized by Rome. Working in conjunction with the Fathers there, a community of Sisters, Handmaids of the Precious Blood, carries on an apostolate of intense Eucharistic prayer combined with active corporal works of mercy. *Via Coeli* is a unique monastery where "priests with problems," chiefly spiritual, live in priestly comradeship and rebuild, in an atmosphere of kindly fraternal charity, in so far as is necessary, health of body and soul. Hundreds of priests pass through this "Way of Heaven" and return to Christ's harvest fields to gather His wheat.

Via Coeli, so far unique, is situated at a great distance from large cities and important dioceses. In time there will be other *Via Coeli's*, here and there throughout our immense country, that will be open always, night and day, to afford a happy shelter, and a blessed home, to every wandering priest who hears Mary's call: "I want you!"

They are ours, all of them, however broken in health and spirit they may be. My one great dream is that all who love Christ should love His homeless priests, and pray and make sacrifices for them, and for their sanctification.

Chapter XVIII

OUR LADY OF RANSOM

AND now I will close this book on a note that is at once personal, and (as I think) mystical.

When I finished my manuscript, that is, up to this final chapter, I was fully conscious of its inadequacy, but also of the fact that I could do no better. I had meant well but all I was able to achieve was a clumsy feeble effort. After sending it to the publisher, I began to fear that my book was ill-advised, and to pray fervently to our Lady that under no circumstances should she allow it ever to see the light of day unless she knew that good would come of it.

Time went by and it seemed to me that my publishers had quite forgotten about me and my book. No doubt they had come to see that it would be unwise to bring out a book of this kind. It became still easier for me to pray: "Dear Mother, unless my book will do good, prevent its publication!"

It was by now September, 1955; close to the end and, indeed, the last Saturday of the month. That morning, at the post office, I was handed a package from my publishers which contained the printed galley proofs of this book.

It was not long before I grasped the significance of this unexpected happening on this particular morning. If you glance back at your calendar you will see that the day was September the twenty-fourth, and the feast of Our Lady of Ransom!

And so it seemed to me that Our Lady of Ransom had decided that good would come of this plea for prayer and sacrifice for the redemption of her captive priests, and that she had, in her kindness, chosen to give me a little sign, which is her way with all of us, that she was pleased.

For the stray shepherd is essentially a captive; a captive of fear, or of confusion of mind, or of human weakness. Like other captives he is confined behind a "curtain," not indeed of iron or bamboo, but of some intangible, sinister material. As in the case of other captives his exact whereabouts are often hidden. His worst sufferings are known to himself alone. Only of two things about him are we certain: he is lonely; he longs to be free.

Compassion for captives and the desire to redeem them, if needs be to ransom them, has always characterized the Church. Back in the early thirteenth century, when great numbers of Christians were held in bondage by Moors and Saracens, Our Lady of Ransom appeared in a vision to St. Peter Nolasco (1189–1256) in Barcelona, Spain, and inspired him to found an Order for the Redemption of Captives. Our Lady is forever moved by the sufferings of her beloved children: that they should be free is her dearest wish.

After his vision St. Peter organized a great crusade of

prayer, sacrifice, and almsgiving. He had, like the Good Shepherd, to seek and find and carry back to safety the prisoners of the Turks. He had to have the means to pay ransoms, for without ransom, in some form or other, captives are not freed.

Stray shepherds are won back from bondage today only when a price has been paid, though the coinage is not gold but prayers and sacrifices. I have known many priests who were once captives, and one and all have told me that the ransom paid for their freedom was prayer and love. I look back on my own life, my twenty years in chains, and I know with a certainty unalloyed by doubt, that the ransom paid for my redemption was made up of the sacrifices, love, and prayers of my true friends.

Captive priests, though they be separated from us in more ways than one, are still our brothers, our relatives, our friends, or, it may be, our beloved benefactors of former times. Here in the United States, there are thousands of Catholics in whose minds the clear image of one or other of them still survives. How many of us are concerned? How many do something for the ransom of his or her friend or relative? Have we no care for that priest of Christ whom we know so well? There are thousands of good souls who pay in full their share of the needed ransom, but are there no (so-called) Catholics who are indifferent about the captive priest, or who are even cruel toward him?

With sorrow and shame I ask, have there not been Catholic employers who, hearing that one of their workers was "a fallen priest," promptly dismissed him and practically drove him onto the streets to starve? Have there not been editors of Catholic papers, who in reviewing some foolish book, written by a priest still victim of his confusions, made public for all the world to read the sins and wrong-doings of the unhappy author so as to discredit him? Does Our Lady of Ransom, who loves her poor captives whatever their faults may be, wish them to be subjected to libel and starvation?

Sometimes we tell with pious contentment the story of the happy death of a homeless priest, but in so doing should we not also strike our breasts?

Not long ago a nun relayed to me by letter the following story. Two Sisters, whom she knew, were helping in a diocesan census and stopped at a lodging-house to inquire of the landlady if she had any Catholic boarders in her house. The woman, who was non-Catholic and somewhat surly toward them, replied that there was an old fellow who was dying in one of her rooms who might be a Catholic. The nuns knocked at the door of this room, and having entered asked the old man who was evidently very ill if he was a Catholic. The old man's sad eyes rested on them and he said: "I am a priest!"

The nuns did everything they could for him; they called a priest and had the joy of seeing him die a good and happy death, reconciled to His Master. But how can we refrain from wondering that one of our priests should have been so forgotten, so neglected as was this poor man? He was a veteran of Christ's army, wounded and in disgrace, but are we to leave such homeless? Need we leave them to die alone?

The other day the great patriot-priest of Eire, Canon J. M. Hayes of Bansha, wrote me in a letter: "The most beautiful death I was privileged to be present at was that of a priest *off the mission*. He was a saint!" But why was the price of his ransom not paid in good time and in full measure? Why must our saints die their holy deaths among strangers?

As I write, visions of many heroic workers in this great cause cross my mind, priests and nuns, men and women of the world, who devote themselves and all they have. There are Nuns in Templemore in Ireland who live up to their name of Mercy, who have initiated a Crusade of Prayer that spreads far and wide. And among the crusaders are scores of priests who offer a Mass each month for the sacred cause of their unhappy brothers. Prayer is all that is needed that the Crusade may be effective, but prayer must be understood in the wide and true sense that embraces action and sacrifice. That I also call prayer, when a priest or layman seeks and finds in some dark corner of a city a worn-out, grief-stricken priest, allays his fears by loving kindness, wins his trust, and brings him home. They are "out there" in the mist: to be found they must be sought: and to be redeemed they must be loved. Is not compassion easy to every soul that hears Mary say: "I want them back"?

It is time for me, now, to bring to a close this last chapter; to write the last page of a book that will be intelligible only to such as have a vivid, realistic faith in Christ and in His priesthood. The life of a priest, an *alter Christus,* is one of danger and of glory. The priest is both the target of devils and the protégé of angels. Often he is wounded, and sometimes he stumbles and falls. Christ foresaw it all — and gave him great faith for his safekeeping.

> Be Thou my vision, O Lord of my heart,
> Naught is all else to me, save that Thou art!
>
> Thou my best thought by day and by night,
> Waking or sleeping, Thy Presence my light.
>
> Be Thou my wisdom, Thou my true word,
> I ever with Thee, Thou with me, Lord!
>
> (Old Irish.)